GW01606709

Alberto Uncini Manganelli

ALBI. MAXI. RICKI.

THREE FRIENDS, ONE GAME

Albi, Maxi, Ricki. Three friends, one game
Original Title: Albi, Maxi, Ricki. Tre amici, un pallone.

Alberto Uncini Manganelli
Massimiliano Tassoni
Riccardo Vigiano

Oohwii SA
Settembre 2021
ISBN 978-2-9701538-4-9
1.01.

Translation: Patrick Kendrick
Graphic Design: Ingrid Wenger

The smell of the grass.

The sound of the studs down the corridor to the locker rooms.

Stories of football in the academy, first team, provincial grounds, unbeatable teams of 11 friends, unlikely events and 5 ACLs.

Both serious and tongue-in-cheek.

Tears of joy and pain.

The poetry of football and its irony become life's metaphors and reveal some universal learning and values, that beyond the personal facts and emotions, will live with us forever.

Albi. Maxi. Ricki.

Three friends, one story.

Three lives, one friendship.

To the teammates. The best friends.

To the coaches. The toughest teachers.

To the parents. The most loyal fans.

THANKS

A special thanks to those who have inspired or helped the creation of this book, with a personal contribution for a social impact:

Ingrid Wenger for the graphic design.

Patrick Kendrick for the translation into the English version.

Nico Tuppen, Ben Millingan e Lauren de Beer for the editing of the English version.

Silvio Trombetta for the editing of the Italian version.

Antonio, Fabio, Francesco A., Francesco G., Max, Paolo, Patrick, Silvio, Stefano, Tom for the time dedicated reading the first draft and for their honest feedback that has given me the courage to continue and the inspiration to improve.

Ricardo and Spencer, for the passion in creating the connection with such great champions that could appreciate the book and share their thoughts and comments.

Marcela Munoz for the support and collaboration with Common Goal

Ivan, head of "Corriere dello Sport", for having dedicated time and inspiration to the foreword that in two intense and wonderful pages capture the spirit, the soul and the values of the story.

All the champions that have dedicated their own time to read and share their thoughts and comments, to help contributing to the charity project.

Everyone called out in this book, for having inspired a story of football, friendship and life, lasting 47 years... for now...

Maxi and Ricki, for a life-long friendship. Ours.

I acknowledge that memory, especially when going deep in the past, may not reflect the events with the best precision, and eventually some timelines may have been slightly misaligned, despite the best intent to reflect the facts as I remember at best today.

ABOUT COMMON GOAL

The Common Goal movement supports high-impact initiatives that use football to drive progress towards the United Nations Global Goals. It encourages professional football players, managers, officials and clubs to donate a minimum of 1% of their earnings to catalyse social change through the beautiful game. In doing so, Common Goal aims to establish an intrinsic link between football as a business and football as a tool for social development and ensure that the game plays its role in tackling the biggest global challenges of our time - from advancing gender equality to driving employment and growth, to promoting greater peace, social justice, supporting underserved communities and the development of children and youth through football.

The movement's long-term vision is to unlock 1% of the entire football industry's revenues — estimated at €50 billion per year — for impact partner organisations that use the game to empower disadvantaged young people and their communities.

Since its inception in August 2017, over 200 professional football players, managers and football executives from over 40 countries have joined - including Paulo Dybala, Pernille Harder, Giorgio Chiellini, Serge Gnabry, Casey Stoney, and Jürgen Klopp. Other influential football figures have joined the movement, such as the UEFA President Aleksander Čeferin, Eric Cantona, plus professional clubs from many leagues in different continents. To date, over €3M has been generated for high-impact football for good initiatives in more than 40 countries.

FOREWORD
BY IVAN ZAZZARONI.

I found long lost friends such Stefano Girotti, known as Speggiorin or Spegg - he always scored. And Moreno, our semi-professional player, who at the age of seventeen ended up at Rosetana in Serie D. And Claudio Gemini, and Jaures the centre back who still calls up on me, and Gallo, and Magrini, and my brother Fabio who played as right fullback.

I have relived the many nights of half sleep, felt again the same anxiety, cultivated the same hopes. Some of the very same questions from those days easily came out from the fog of time: will it rain? And how much will it rain? Will the thunderstorms end up making the pitch unplayable and will the football association – so dry and insensitive – therefore suspend the championship? No, please don't make it snow. And anyway, how long does this annoying winter last? I want to play, it's my whole young life, I want to wake up early on Sunday morning, with the bag ready, go down to the bar where we usually meet for our short yet endless away trip. I want it, I want spring back, the first heat, the smell of freshly cut grass, the path from the locker room to the pitch, sometimes very short, chest out like a little gladiator. I looked at the standings, today the opponents are strong. In my lost diary there was everything, in this book there is even more. Football from age six to eighteen, "because afterwards - as Chiari told me - it will no longer be the same. With the end of the youth teams the best season ends”. That of football in its purest form.

I have imagined the goal I will score this morning at least twenty times. Like Alberto and his two friends. The Dozza, the Sparta, the Bo.Ca, the San Lazzaro, the try outs with Roma, Massese, Empoli, Sambenedettese and me, who naively thought that I had to reach San Benedetto Val di Sambro, instead it was San Benedetto del Tronto.

In a crescendo that never loses concreteness thanks to the many involuntary accomplices and timeless friendships, this book of passion and feelings tells of a world and moments and figures that belong to hundreds of professionals, to millions of fans, to former boys. Alberto's memory manages to capture us to the very end and then evaporates into a smile tinged with bitterness, even the smile of the infinite dream. “The dream of every player (shared by every spectator) is to start from the middle of the pitch, dribble everyone and score” wrote Pasolini. “If, within the limits allowed, one can imagine something sublime in football, it is precisely this. But it never happens.”

Today we are the way we are also thanks to that football, to those days, to those emotions. Before we went looking for life outside, we had found it inside the game.

Ivan Zazzaroni

"Football has always been a part of my life. I don't remember a day going by when football wasn't there in some way.

Like any humble family, we had many hardships during my childhood, and it turned out to be the path I wanted to follow. I never thought of sport as a way to earn money, but as my journey, my destiny and always next to my family and to God.

The book tells how friendship, barriers and achievements define the pillars that will shape us in today's men. For those who love this sport and have practiced it at any level, it is impossible to not identify oneself and to not get excited. Great reading!"

Cafu

"We all have different reasons for relating to the greatest sport in the world. We build connections that transform teammates into our family, where we adopt whoever will genuinely be by our side.

In this game, we face barriers that make us grow up and prepare us for a life of challenges. And it is with this game that we mould the pillars that make us more human. The ball forces us to be creative, to be competitive, to have discipline in a playful and spontaneous way.

In the pages of this book, we find these elements that identify and unite all those who live the passion for football."

Kaka

"The book is wonderful, it shows that football is open to everyone, and that football (as life) is about merit, takes a lot of passion, actions,

blood and tears, and that you need to give it your very best... Sometimes, as in life, you must accept the uncontrollable.

Some people try to reduce sports only to a mechanical and theoretical thing, while it takes life, career and emotional management, study, competence, and you need to have principles and values.

It's made of morals, of ethical standards, and, most importantly, of emotions."

Dunga

"The world's most popular sport has its own mysteries. We will never know with certainty what's the magic that brings this miracle to life.

Football is a teacher and transforms us and our human relationships.

It's dream, it's entertainment, it's ethic, it's aesthetic, it's friendship. This book is an additional proof that if us humans were able to create this game that teaches so much to everyone, it's because there is hope. There is hope in life!"

Raî

"This book is able to tell people the true emotion that football offers, inside and outside the pitch. The belonging, the joy, the sadness, all those feelings lived through sport!

It's incredible!"

Adriano

"The amazing thing about this book is the fact that while you're reading it, you can imagine yourself as one of the three friends. There are so many situations, feelings, thoughts recounted that we could read pieces of our lives in the story. And about this, it's always incredible how much football creates connections between us. It creates friendships, it creates memories, it creates equality. This is the concept on which Common Goal is based, a project that through this sport tackles current social problems."

Claudia Ferrato

"This book is a great story about friendship, perseverance and doing what you love. Those are key aspects that drives me as a sportsman."

Wayde van Niekerk

"A trip down memory lane. It is a really interesting read that brings back a lot of memories for me. Going through the stories of the three friends and their journeys in football, took me back to my soccer days and rituals that I used to have. He got a lot from football, more than just the enjoyment of it. It was part of his life that left him with lifelong friends, a drive to always give your best in everything you do and a whole flux of emotions that will never leave. "

Akani Simbine

INTRODUCTION

I dreamed of winning the World Cup. Maxi was only interested in playing football. Ricki loved the aesthetics of the Beautiful Game.

There is more than one side to every story.

This is a tale about football, friendship and, more in general, about life's experiences that transcend the facts. Those personal emotions and feelings that football provides reveal deeper reflections and define some universal values that may emerge from playing the game, but they go beyond football.

It's a story that begins with football as seen through the eyes of three kids, who meet aged six and just love kicking a ball around. Football that creates emotions equally unforgettable as undefinable, and that they come flooding back, unstoppable, many years later.

The story evolves through friendship, which stands the test of time and that goes beyond the events.

But besides the specific facts, the story, just like football, finds a real purpose and perhaps its real value, as a pathway for pursuing life's lessons and realizing the general principles that serve everyone's life.

The discovery that certain moments and certain opportunities will change things forever. Those differences which are barely perceptible one day become massive a decade later. Those few seconds or few inches that will mean the difference between winning and losing. The formula – undefinable - that combines talent, will power, and opportunity, that shapes everything in sport, as well as in personal and professional life. Those failures and those scars that will leave a much bigger mark on the inside than the outside.

I wanted to become a World Champion.

It was my dream. In fact, at that team, it was sounding to me more like a real plan.

So, this is the tale of a dream that didn't come true, or a goal never achieved. But the journey provides us with so many lessons and it tells us that there are always fewer doors that close behind you than there are ones that open in front of you.

This personal account, full of the joy of a child's perspective and many missed opportunities along the way, is not the end but merely a starting point. It is a means of capturing some thoughts about what unites and drives all of the Albis, Maxis and Rickis who have ever run around on a football pitch. Whether or not they made it in the game is but a footnote, a minor detail, because when football is over - and sooner or later that time comes for everyone - what you're left with inside is what matters the most.

So, the only thing left to ask is: What remains of our football?

1. ALBI
2. MAXI
3. RICKI
4. THE SMELL OF THE GRASS
5. PLAYING FOREVER
6. THE FIRST MATCH
7. WORLD CUP '82
8. THE UNBEATABLES
9. "ESORDIENTI" (*) ON THE PITCH AND IN LIFE (*UNDER 12)
10. COACHES, TEAMS AND ROLES
11. GIOVANISSIMI** (**UNDER 14)
12. PARTING WAYS
13. EVERYTHING CHANGES IN 3 DAYS: TRIALS, KISSES, LIGAMENTS
14. THE BLUE CLIO
15. THE TEAM '92- '98
16. RAFFA'S JUMPS
17. A SAD SHOOTOUT
18. "GRAZIA"... AND TALENT
19. WAGSx
20. LIGAMENTS
21. COMEBACKS
22. THE PITCH... AND THE PITCHES
23. CHOICES
24. WHAT REMAINS OF OUR FOOTBALL?
25. EXTRA-TIMES AND PENALTIES

ALBI

Some stories can't be told. Or you can try to tell them, but it's unlikely to bring them to life in a way that makes them truly understood.

Some feelings belong to a level of consciousness which is neither physical nor mental, yet they are emotions that get under your skin without passing through the logical filter of the brain.

And you are stuck with them. They will never leave.

They are just there, forever, in a corner of your memory, and, sometimes, of your soul.

But when several of us have experienced those same emotions on the football pitch, you share those feelings as easily as via Bluetooth or Airdrop. In a fraction of a second you can transfer a whole world as if by osmosis and without even describing it. And if you say to a 40-year-old the two simple words, "Tigre conditioner," you have opened the door to an entire world of feelings, transferring in wireless emotions and memories that would take you days to explain.

Gigabytes, maybe even terabytes, in a fraction of a second.

But you can't explain it to someone who hasn't experienced it. They just wouldn't get it. It's as if they're separated by a firewall.

It's the funny irony about football that to the wonder, the intensity, and the emotion of when you score a goal opposes the impossibility to share how it feels. That moment, that shiver, that energy.

A goal is a shockwave that for who lives it will remain impossible to tell. Unless you've lived it, you'll never understand. What courses through your veins and your mind in that moment, as the goal goes in, remains a mystery. It's a force that surges from the dark – uncontrolled - and uncontrollable. It's a rush that appears out of nowhere which can banish fatigue, zeroing any brain activity, while taking your breath away.

It's overpowering. It's unique. It's totalizing.

Like catching the eye of that cute blonde girl in middle school that will take away your breath, as well as your appetite for weeks on end.

In the same way you can't describe those fleeting glances you give one another in the locker room at half time. A break that's always too long in the winter, so that you'll be freezing when back on the pitch until about seven minutes into the second half. But also too short to get to the bottom of how in hell that number 11 managed to beat three of ours without anyone fouling him. And where on earth was Maxi?

It's the Dubbin from the night before that you carefully applied to your adidas World Cups, that shimmer with those new metal studs. Can someone tell me please who has given the firearm license to all central defenders in the second division?

And for sure those red stripes on the outsole of the world cup shoes are really cool but what actual use are they? I don't want to know, and I score goals anyway so that's fine with me.

It's the smell of freshly cut grass.

It's the dew on a Sunday morning (which naturally is completely different to the dew on any other day), that squirts all the way up your shorts and soaks your pants as soon as you make your first slide tackle 3 minutes into the match.

It's the sound of studs in the tunnel from the locker rooms – that's the soundtrack to football.

It's that glass of tea at half time which for some unknown reason is always too cold in the winter and too hot in the summer. Always zero flavour but you can't wait to hold it with both your hands, and the elbows on the knees.

It's that strip of white tape to hold your shin pads just above the ankle, that breaks up the colour of your socks. Later, with the advance of technology it could be replaced by a lightweight, translucent elastic band that you could wrap around your shin pads without the need for tape and so it could come into contact with the skin. It was also known as "skin saver." I actually used a wrap just below the kneecap though: first one round of "skin saver" then the white tape precisely twice around my leg. It was more a ritual than a need. Anyway, I was better off keeping my knee in position, you never know. I wanted to avoid doing my ACL again.

I know. It will work.

And let's be honest, no one gives massages like Giorgione.

That is, if you're able to get back up again.

And maybe next time we could go a bit easier on the gel because when I get up, I feel my back on fire. I won't stop scratching the small of my back until a quarter of an hour into the game.

I started on the right wing as a kid. At that time, I used to pick up the ball and dribble past everyone. Every time. And not really because of incredible skills, but because mother nature gifted me with two long legs, longer than the average of my peers. I could kick the ball and run after it faster than anyone else (I had to learn a lot more in the following years when that trick couldn't work anymore). Then I would be able to cross the ball into the middle with enough precision that it only needed a touch to score a goal.

As a right winger and striker I scored lots of goals and I set up even more. At that time all that mattered to me was playing for Italy and winning the World Cup.

It wasn't a dream.

It was a plan.

In order to turn me into a "footballer", one coach picked me at left-back in a team of guys who were two years older for a whole season. At that age, two years was a lot. I wasn't thrilled about it, but he had great intuition.

And then I became a central midfielder or sometimes a bit wider, but I was always more attack-minded, usually scoring 10-15 goals a season, including penalties and free-kicks. One season I bagged 18 goals and hit the bar 11 times from set-pieces.

I like playing strategies, clean geometries, triangles, tidy passing, the diagonals in the zone midfield play scheme, crossfield balls and those through balls that in the space of two touches put someone through on goal. Still today I can see invisible trajectories and love going vertical in two touches.

In 72 hours, when I just turned 18, I lived the emotion of competing well at the professional level, of finding that love that will define all my adult life, while letting go dreams that were bigger than my talent. In the same 3 days I started to understand the importance of being focused on the doors opening in front, rather than the one closing behind.

Some moments, connected with the pitch, with playing football and with the team, have provided learning and set some values that transcend the pitch, and they go beyond football, influencing many other life experiences. Many episodes and circumstances that have forged attitudes now indivisible from our personality, writing who we are, defining who we will become or suggesting what we will teach to our kids.

Back into the pitch, the rituals are still the same.

You line up when you walk onto the pitch and I'm first up when I'm captain. Otherwise, I try to be the last on, but I have to compete with Ricki.

I wear the armband on my right arm, not my left. That might be because I wear a separate armband on my left elbow which covers up the 30 stitches on my elbow, the result of an overhead kick which went very badly wrong when I was only 13. That's why I've never been a big fan of the number 13.

But I love number 17 - my number in the list at primary school - way back when my main concern was only about beating the team from the years above. Those numbers were irrelevant to the match because at that time, in real football, the only ones that truly mattered were 1 to 11. So, for me all that mattered were the number 7, 8, 9, 10 and 11 shirts. And, for one season, number 3.

I only tie the laces on my boots when I'm out on the pitch – never in the dressing room. I don't know why.

I would meticulously prepare for a penalty by placing my left foot next to the ball and then taking exactly three and a half steps back. The half step was crucial too. It was more of a ritual than technique.

But I scored every single one of them. For 15 years. Every year. Apart from one. And you're trying to tell me to change my approach.

Everyone has their own rituals.

I've seen the lot in terms of players: well-travelled footballers, experienced players, youngsters with great talent, with lots of goals and trophies won and even the odd broken nose on their CV. But they all fall into the trap of rituals. All of them.

At the very least a quick scratch of the balls for good luck when the referee says, "Have a good game," after the name check. Just to be safe.

There's no rhyme or reason for these rituals. Or maybe there is something supernatural about football that we don't want to get to the bottom of. Because you might get hurt. What if you discover that if you stop tying your laces on the pitch you end up losing control of every ball? And what if you miss a penalty? And how about if an easy pass goes straight to the opposition? It's too risky. Plus, in Serie A you see guys walking out with three skips on their right leg, so I reckon I can tie my laces on the pitch and smell the grass. If there is any grass.

I still do it today when I put on my running shoes. Never at home but always on the road, kneeling down, perhaps because it takes me back to the football pitch even now. Again. One more time.

That's why I roll up the sleeves on my shirt or pull up the sleeves on my long-sleeve T-shirts in the office before the start of the first meeting. Every day.

As if to say: "Ready, away we go."

MAXI

Let's get one thing straight: I've never been that fussed about football on TV. Ever since I was a kid, I've supported Bologna and I still follow them, but I'm not fanatical. During training, everyone used to talk about the results from the previous weekend or from the Champions League, about that amazing curler from Alessandro Del Piero. But I didn't feel a part of it. I stayed out of it. Apart from the Italian team.

You cannot touch the Azzurri.

Maybe I follow it more closely now that I no longer play, and I've realised why that is. When I played the game, that was the only football in my eyes. Football matches were always an outlet for my most aggressive self-expression. It was a time and a space of freedom. End of story.

I would go into battle, and I felt like a warrior. It was a fight till the death.

I loved slide tackles – committed - clean ones when you take the whole ball. I was as brave when going to ground as I was precise. I didn't just hope to take the ball; I knew I would. And the defender hoped so too, because just a few inches higher would have meant several weeks on the treatment table for the striker and several weeks' suspension for me.

In truth I took the ball a lot more than I did opponents' ankles, and I didn't get too many red cards–something fairly unusual for a stopper or a centre-half.

But I would end up cursing those slide tackles later that night in bed, when I would accidentally roll and then lie on my side where the skin had been scraped away and the bedsheets would stick to me like the Pritt-stick I used in primary school.

Luckily over the years I found a solution to that issue thanks to a "silver spray" as it was named; a big breakthrough in the world of medicine.

It was never my dream to become a professional footballer.

I played because I liked football and it felt good.

I enjoyed it basically, that was it.

I've always been great at giving it all. Hard work never bothered me. I've always been a good, diligent soldier who used to listen to the coach and do his job, sometimes without even realising in detail what was happening on the pitch because I was so utterly focused on two things: the ball and my opponent. Those two things were all that existed for 90 minutes plus added time.

That was until I turned 15 and I learned more about the game when we moved to zonal marking and that opened my eyes to a whole new world. The game had changed completely and with it so had my position.

Up until that point, besides the odd appearance at right-back, I had always played as a centre-back or a man marker, until the age of 15 as

I said. I think I was one of the only kids who idolised Pietro Vierchowod. I doubt young people these days even know who he is, so they're probably unaware of one of the best defenders in the history of Italian football. A gutsy brick wall of a defender, blessed with an impressive engine and the ability to read the game and the opponent like no one else. Apart from maybe Fabio Cannavaro. Pietro Vierchowod was one of the heroes of the great Sampdoria side of Gianluca Vialli and "il Mancio." He even won the 1982 World Cup without ever featuring, plus two leagues' titles with Roma and Sampdoria.

I've always thought that man marking someone is one of the easiest positions there is because you always know what to look for: the centre-forward. The first thing you do is to take a look at him. You see whether he's right- or left-footed, if he's quicker than you or not and from his build you can figure out whether he likes to run in behind or whether he's less mobile because he's got good feet. Job done. Or rather you need to grab hold of his shirt or shorts for the remainder of the 90 minutes and never switch off even for a fraction of a second. Use your hands, arms, elbows, legs and head to make sure he doesn't get a look at the ball. He mustn't ever see it. End of discussion.

Sometimes, when there was an odious striker, I'd literally hand him the ball when walking back down the tunnel towards the locker room after the match. Now he could finally touch it.

When you man mark someone in some games you might only get 10 touches on the ball, of which 9 aren't clean, because you always intercepted the ball playing in advance to the opponent. Two of those balls will end up in row Z.

So, you needed to have the utmost concentration. Ten touches in 90 minutes, each of them a split second's difference between winning and losing.

For me, a gladiator, it was about living or dying.

That was always the position I called my own. I was quick, I always used to intercept the ball and I realised I was pretty good at it too.

But when you play as a man marker you inevitably become a bit detached from the rest of the team, because once you win the ball back you play it to your nearest teammate and that's often where your involvement ends. You aren't a big part of the build-up play. That's why I wasn't exactly sure of what went on ahead of me, between midfield and the forward line.

That all changed at 15.

The Bologna academy developed us as players until we were 14 and that's when it ended. From time to time, I think about how much more fun I could have had with my teammates from those unforgettable years. We could have played together until we were 17 and then joined a senior side. But that's where our dreams ended and many of us went our separate ways. I signed for Boca-Sparta.

I still remember pre-season training that August. It was absolutely exhausting; with the most intense sessions I'd ever seen. It ran like clockwork; the coaches all wore stopwatches round their necks and the sessions were punctuated by short, sharp blasts of the whistle.

But what struck me the most was the amount of tactical work we'd do on the whiteboard. They told us that season–from the first team down to us Under-15s–we would all play zonal marking. It was all change. It had been seen in Serie A for a few years by that stage. Arrigo Sacchi had built the great AC Milan side with the Dutch trio, while in Serie B Gigi Maifredi (with an even bolder take of the same methodology) led Bologna to a record-breaking season.

I didn't really know what it meant. You no longer man marked your opponent, but you picked up the one closest to you – that was how I understood it.

I remember that we spent hours in front of the magnetic whiteboard, where there were 11 circles that made up the formation and time after time, they would show us how the back four and midfield lines would move together. As a unit as much as possible, always perfectly in line with one another, narrow when defending, wide when you win the ball back. It was the first time that spacing became crucial, as if we were all tied to a rubber band.

Then on the pitch, they lined us up in the back 4 and handed us a long rope running from right to left and they had us run and move while holding onto the rope, to make us see that we were all one single unit.

I found it interesting this concept of maintaining distances, to occupy all spaces in the most effective and balanced way. I found it practical, many years later, in personal relationships as well as in the family life.

I very quickly came to enjoy the new system. I finally figured out how the midfield and forward lines operated and how the shape of one area of the pitch had an impact on the others. Finally, we were trying to build out from the back. I was no longer a man marker but a centre-back in a zonal marking scheme. A much cooler position. But above all I played football and I actively contributed to possession as opposed to simply making sure the opposition didn't get the ball. So, I would create play rather than stopping my opponents from doing so.

It was an exciting prospect. Two amazing things happen when you switch from man marking to zonal. First you gain an extra man, the sweeper, thus having greater numbers in the middle of the park and creating an overload and way more density where the centre of the play is.

Then the centre-backs automatically become deep-lying playmakers, so it became a completely different game. It was a new whole position. You needed different attributes. And yes, you needed to be good on the ball. Winning the ball and clearing your lines – sometimes straight into touch – would no longer cut it. I only played in that system for four years. When I was 18, I started university and I decided to re-unite with Albi and Ricki, where the coach was preferring a man-marking system. Albi came back a few months later because he'd done his ligaments the previous year.

For me playing that position again was like taking a step back – tracking the striker from left to right, following him in the box and into midfield with no rhythm to my game. It meant running a lot more, it was more mentally draining, and you would have 10 touches on the ball over the course of a match. It was like not playing football at all. You couldn't even go up for corners because they all wanted me to stay back tight to my man or stay as a spare man ready to nip in and snuff out any potential counterattack: "Maxi, stay back because you're quick."

My relationship with football can be broken down into three very distinct phases and they were all eye-opening experiences: Discovering football in all its simplicity; making lifelong friendships; and learning the systems and formations which turn football from a fairly random game into an exact science.

I stopped playing football competitively at 22. I was coming to the end of university and giving up my Sundays to stay back on corners started to irritate me. I wanted greater freedom. I'd lost that ambition, but most of all I started to lose that will to win. That competitive drive. The feeling you get as you fall asleep the night before a game.

I stopped playing football altogether for 3 years, apart from the odd tournament or a 7-a-side game on a Sunday. In 1999 I started playing again in an amateur team until I was 37. Then it was all 7-a-side until I was 41, alongside Ricki. Then after I ruptured my cruciate ligaments in my right knee for the second time following another painful period of recovery, I called it quits. During those last years of playing, we even managed to play a match together, all of three of us: myself, Ricki, and Albi, who had travelled back from Switzerland on the Friday so that he could play with us.

It felt great. Let's face it, Albi was in tip-top shape and on his game because he'd started playing seriously again in Geneva. He scored with a free kick that left the opposition keeper clutching at thin air.

It was nice to be back together: the three of us; the meeting point; the car drive to the pitch; the smell of Deep Heat; the match, the scalding hot shower; Albi always asking for the shower gel (exactly as in the past 40 years); our talks; a pub in via Andrea Costa.

RICKI

I've been playing football for as long as I can remember, anytime, anywhere. At home with a makeshift ball of rolled-up newspaper and masking tape. The TV stand was the goal and the tape recorder the keeper - static yet imposing. I broke the lot at home, anything you can imagine, and my mum knew that it wasn't the cat, however much I tried to convince her of that.

Then came the sponge ball and with it more damage.

I often used to play on my own in the garden, commentating on myself and shooting towards goal - my garden gate - while chased by excellent defenders, my dogs.

I would spend my summers on La Maddalena and not just the summer either. My friends and I would graze our knees on every patch of ground and all we needed was a bit of room and the pitch very quickly transformed into our Bernabeu – whether it was "il campo dei Colmi," "il campo del Pastore," or the one at the end of "Via Chiusedda." Video games and tablets hadn't been invented yet, so we just wandered around with a ball tucked under our arms looking for a patch of grass or sand and two makeshift posts, fueled by an unconditional love for the Beautiful Game.

Football has given me so much – massive highs and awful lows. But above all it introduced me to my best friends – proper friends. I met some of my closest mates on a football pitch or in the dressing room, at every age and various stages of my life. That's because you never stop playing football. Things change, the pitches get smaller and your waistband gets bigger, yet there you are still chasing after the ball just as you did when you were seven years old, eyes wide and full of wonder.

That's how I met Maxi and Albi, aged around 6 or 7, on a pitch in the Barca district of Bologna where we used to train. We all wore red and blue kits, a group of kids who shared the same passion and desire to meet people and learn new things. And play football of course. I can vividly remember my first meeting with Albi - I don't even know why but it's clearly one of those flashbacks to the past that stay lodged in your mind. He was a tall kid with freckles, brown hair, a good right foot and with a gifted elegance to how he moved on the pitch. They paired us together to do one of those warm-up drills that were all the rage among coaches back then: instep, laces, chest and instep, right foot, left foot. I looked at him without knowing then that he would go on to become one of my closest friends. Nor did I realize that despite fate taking us to different parts of the world we would tackle all of life's challenges together, sharing joy and pain, and that 15 years later he would introduce me to my wife, the mother of my children. No, at that moment we were just two focused little boys, careful not to misplace passes to our teammates, to try to bring out the best of one another. And to be honest he never put a foot wrong. I can picture him with a hint of a grin on his face, holding the ball, ready to throw it to me. When several years go by your memory takes the form of a moment – a snapshot – a picture tied to a feeling and a mindset. And that's where it remains.

And Albi, like Maxi, has stayed there.

The three of us began playing football at a young age. The squad changed a great deal in the years after that. Some kids gave up football and, as is only natural when you're 6, 7 or 10 years old, others changed sport. Some of the guys joined because they moved from somewhere else or because they took up football a bit later. Then there were those who signed from other teams. At that age, when you're a child or moving into your teens, coaches are the people you look up to. They show you the way and not only when it comes to sport. They are often role models in terms of behavior, first the basic tenets of sportsmanship on the pitch and then how to conduct yourself off it too. Coaches are second only to your home life and school.

That bunch of kids, in the "Esordienti" age group (under 12), for some strange, unknown reason became a brilliant football team.

Our academy was created under the protective arm of Bologna FC, the great Bologna, the team we all supported. That meant we were lucky enough to have Cesarino Cervellati as technical director and Mirko Pavinato as coach, both icons of the game in Bologna. We were the ones who would walk out onto the pitch before Bologna games, lining up one behind the other and holding hands to form a giant B in the final home match of the season, as Bologna got promoted into Serie A from the second tier. That was at the Stadio Comunale which would later be renamed the Renato Dall'Ara. It was 1984, we were 10 years old, and like every kid we all hoped to be back on that pitch a few years later as stars in our own right.

The "Esordienti" season was a success from start to finish. At the end of that campaign a number of us were selected for trials at Bologna. I turned up to Casteldebole for a match along with lots of other kids from across the Bologna area. They were no doubt the guys that had performed best in the various leagues that year and clearly the results of our "unbeatable team" had not gone unnoticed. I was so excited and as nervous as someone just before the World Cup final. There were some excellent players there and some of them looked a lot older than 12. I barely had a kick; I didn't enjoy it one bit and a few days later they told some of the players from our team that they had been selected by Bologna. They would train on the Bologna pitches, at the training ground in Casteldebole and wear the famous Rossoblù colors with the sponsor and everything the following season. I was not one of them.

That was my chance to jump aboard, yet the train of opportunity flashed before my eyes as I bid farewell to my teammates that climbed on. As I was walking to the car on the way home from the match, in the car park at Casteldebole, I heard a voice shouting, "Ricki! Ricki!" I turned around and saw Franco Bonini, our supervisor for want of a better word; a wise, charismatic man, someone we'd all listen to in silence when he spoke. Mr. Bonini smiled at me and said, "Hey Ricki, remember you're the best player here and things will go better next time." I found a smile amid my sadness, a smile full of disenchantment and disappointment.

The following year our team was no longer unbeatable and those of us that remained knew that the best guys were playing elsewhere.

We still played for another two seasons at the academy. Our club only had a youth system until the "Giovanissimi" (under 14) age group and then everyone was let go after that. That meant some guys would have to settle, while others could join a team with prospects.

We had so much fun that last year. We were a group of young lads, all mates and we struck upon the perfect blend on the pitch. A mix of talent and execution. Everyone knew what to do and did their job well. The substitutes weren't really reserves – we didn't really have a second string that season. We were all equally important and all match winners in our own different ways.

Our last match together was the final of the "Savena" tournament, a summer competition that meant a lot in Bologna. It was an important tournament with a big following and was held on a ground that is no longer there. For those of us that played there though, that ground was special; it was synonymous with amateur football, a dust bowl with parents watching on from the stands. The "Savena" tournament was one of the best-known competitions in Bologna, a trophy that everyone wanted to win. We beat Casalecchio in the final 4-1, even though they were the better team on paper and had played in the regional league whereas we had competed in the provincial one. I scored twice and I was hardly a goal scorer – I never have been. It was a moment of indescribable joy: a group of friends lifting an important trophy (it was significant to us) after one wonderful final season together.

It was a moment when you are "full"- in its precise meaning - of joy, that pure happiness that only a 13-year-old can experience.

Football has always been the fun side of my life, the playful part. When you lace up your boots and walk onto the pitch, there's no time for anything else. The game becomes all-consuming, and it occupies your whole mind – there's no room for anything else. You are focused on where the ball goes, how your teammates and opponents move and what you must do and when. Any problem, whether big or small, does not go onto the pitch with you. You leave them on the sidelines. That happens above all when you find yourself on a small pitch in a built-up area in your hometown on a Monday night after work: 40 years of age, with a fading six-pack and dozens of plasters that just about keep the memory of your younger football's physique intact.

All your problems drift away in that hour: bills that are due; young kids; the argument at home a little earlier; your parents who are getting older as you stop being their son and find yourself having to look after them. You spend an hour in your safe place, a very powerful natural antidepressant. A solitary hour to recharge the batteries, with the church bells clearly marking the time. In the midst of the Covid-19 pandemic, when football grounds were closed for several months, it really brought home how much we missed the game as a means of socializing, fitness, wellbeing and blowing off steam.

Football has given me so much, but it hasn't spared me some very painful, sad chapters in my life.

On Boxing Day 2004 the world was rocked by a huge tragedy. An underground earthquake in the Indian Ocean caused a tsunami that hit the coast of South-East Asia as far as Africa - from Indonesia to the Maldives and even Kenya. 200,000 people died in one of the biggest natural disasters of the last 60 years.

I was on my island in Sardinia back then, on La Maddalena, to spend Christmas with my family and a bit of time with my dad. I had a nasty bout of flu. I remember it perfectly; I had a high fever and my grandmother Enza who was looking after me was naturally very worried. The following evening, 27 December, I was in bed when my teammate Marco called me. It was late, too late to be calling someone. Marco could barely get the words out as he told me that during training, the traditional first session back during the winter break, Gino had felt unwell and collapsed to the ground. He told me that despite attempts to resuscitate him, first from my teammates and then the paramedics, it was no use. It was a huge tragedy, a wave that hit us with tremendous force, changing our little world forever. We really struggled to come to terms with what had happened. Some of the guys gave up football at the end of the season and all of us still carry that open wound around with us. I felt very guilty for a long time about not being there on the pitch, with the others, my teammates and friends – I was the captain of that side. Even now, years later, I struggle to come to terms with the magnitude of that event. A strong, handsome young man all of a sudden was no longer with us. Gino was a good-looking guy, a real hunk, and I still remember his almost sheepish, cheeky grin.

They call them sudden deaths because you can't legislate for them, they just happen, and they have even happened to professional players in Serie A. You read about them in the papers and they seem so far off. Yet Gino was close, very close to home. He was the clean-cut guy that used to change next to you in the dressing room; the guy you used to go to watch Bologna with; the one whose flat you went round to for dinner after training because he lived on his own in a small place around the corner from the training ground that he'd bought with his savings and that was his pride and joy. He was a friend. And then one day, all of a sudden, he was no longer there laughing and joking around. He had gone on his way and left his smile behind.

Towards the end of January, we resumed action on the same pitch where it happened. Wearing the captain's armband, my teammates and I laid a wreath of flowers before kick-off on the area of the running track where he had felt unwell, where Gino had collapsed. We were all distraught with pain, incredulous and perhaps even frightened. Endless silences in the dressing room, once a place of laughter and joy, now a place of pain.

I remember that Sunday we conceded after only a few minutes and gradually with every passing minute we tried to find some semblance of normality – an impossible task. And ever since that day, every time I play football, be it a league game or a kickabout with my mates, Gino is always there in the back of my mind.

I remember one year we went to play a fairly run-of-the-mill game on the outskirts of Imola. It was a long, narrow pitch surrounded by factories in an industrial area. It all got a bit tense, and tempers began to flare. Our opponents were behind us in the table but comfortably in midtable, whereas we knew that with a win we could still hope to finish third or make a play-off. Either way a third-place finish would have been a good season. I remember that there could have only been around a meter between the touchline and the fencing. It was so tight and I'm not even sure it was legal. It was a very hard-fought match. We were trailing 2-1 when I went to take a throw on the left wing. An opposition player stood in front of me right on the touchline. I couldn't even take the throw because this guy was right in my face and he would match me stride for stride, side to side. Nor could I backpedal because of the fence behind me. I flagged it up to the referee, but he didn't intervene so in a moment of anger and frustration I threw the ball in my opponent's face. Obviously, I was sent off despite my best efforts to explain myself.

We were down to 10 men and 2 minutes from time when we won a free kick. Our center-back smashed one into the top corner to make it 2-2 to spark wild celebrations on the pitch and by the bench. The referee blew for full time a few minutes later and we celebrated in the dressing room together having secured a point late on – the best way to do it. We couldn't find the coach, no one had seen him. He just disappeared. One of the senior management found him later wandering across a roundabout on his way back to Bologna. From

Imola. On foot. He said he lost his train of thought after the game and began walking home, still in a trance and extremely confused.

After a few years of dating my girlfriend, I realized where football stood in my list of life's priorities and Francesca made a deal with me: I could keep playing for as long as my body held up, but in return I had to promise her I'd never go into coaching. She must've seen the risk of having to always share me with something that could get out of hand. She clearly realized that would mean no shelf life. I stopped playing competitively (in the 8th tier) when I was 35 at the end of the season, in the year my daughter was born. That was the right decision, because I found it so hard to go training in the evenings with a new-born baby at home. There's always a right place for you to be, in the pitch as in life, and you're not always there at the right time.

But it was also the year I took a gamble in football. I played for 2 sides at non-league level and in both instances I was able to move up a division without ever being relegated. That year at Saragozza we had to battle to stay in the 8 division and we managed it. In fact, I had already decided a year earlier to hang up my boots. I hadn't done pre-season and I didn't attend training, but over time I was champing at the bit to get back out there, and I came back into the fold in October even though I couldn't fully commit. The coach only picked me in the cup (which in the 9th tier in Bologna is known as the Predieri Trophy).

As a center-back you don't need to be really quick, nor do you need to be particularly fit – most of the play in that position comes down to experience and positional sense. And that's just what I did in what was supposed to be my last year, as the team's "old timer." Things didn't go that well at the weekends, where we finished midtable in the league – nothing to write home about in the 9th division. But on Wednesday evenings in the cup, the team was transformed and gradually, round by round, we began to believe. We defeated all the teams in our league in knockout format, including the team that finished top and then we began to face the sides that won their respective leagues and had made it through. We won both legs of the semi-final against Marzabotto and that gave us the belief that we were a match for anyone. They were top of the mountain section, traditionally one of the hardest leagues in the Bologna area. So that put us into the final on 25 April 2009 where we faced a top side, your typical team that had been put together with players dropping down the divisions to secure instant success. And needless to say, they won the league. The fact that they had finished top meant that we knew we would be promoted regardless of the result in that final. But we still wanted to win. We wanted to lift the trophy. And so did they. It was a very hard-fought contest, a real battle. It went to sudden death in a penalty shootout: they missed theirs and we scored ours, so we were left to lift the cup. I can't remember an afternoon with more smiles and tears of joy than that one. Our team had been put together a few years earlier by a far-sighted president who had taken a group of old friends and made a side out of them. It was the exact opposite of what usually happens when teammates eventually become friends. So Saragozza, named after an apartment in a Bologna street of the same name, won a trophy.

The following year we stayed up and that was my gamble. I quit playing at the end of the season.

In the years following, that the same enlightened club president asked me if I'd like to coach the team. I felt very honored to be offered the role and I was even tempted. I felt I had learned lots from years of training, games and interacting with people in the dressing room. And I would have liked to have tried it, to see how much I had learned and how much I could offer a group of players. But you must always keep your word, so I reverted to being a dad and allowed myself the odd evening of 5-a-side with friends – the delight of all orthopedists.

I spent the last few years with the Bologna lawyers' side: a team of colleagues of various ages who travel around Italy to take on other lawyers from towns and cities up and down the country. The domestic league is always very competitive and the standard is higher than you might expect. Then you have post-match drinks where the home team puts on a bit of a spread. That becomes the highlight of the event when football brings people together and is almost an excuse to spend time with each other and get to know one another. That's where new friendships are forged.

And in 2009 we became Italian champions and had the Scudetto sewn onto our shirts.

So, what has football left me with?

Football has left me with the true friendships, ones that developed without any second thoughts, rivalry, or opportunism. Guys who became friends while wearing shorts, covered in sweat, tired, and caked in mud. It's left me with thousands of scars and countless niggles.

I still recall the happiness of a Sunday night, the result of all that running in the game that afternoon, an intoxicating form of fatigue.

I still have some medals and awards gathering dust in the cellar, that I recall with the same pride as the day I received them and held them aloft.

I am left with the knowledge that I didn't only chase and kick around a ball. What I did was a form of expression, it was my way of telling the world who I was. It was one of the ways – perhaps even the truest form – of figuring out who you really were.

On the football pitch we all begin on an even footing – it doesn't matter who you are, what you do, how nice you are or how successful you are at work, with friends or with women. What matters is your willingness to work hard for your team, how ready you are to take risks and whether you can summon that last ounce of energy because the game is not yet over, they've won the ball back in midfield and they're running at your defenders.

As a much wiser man than me once said, "In front of our life, we are all wearing football shorts."

THE SMELL OF THE GRASS

Maxi, Ricki, and I met at 6 years old. That day stands strong in my memory, as one of the most special days of my childhood. It was the first day as "Pulcino del Bologna" (in Italian "Pulcino" literally means "Chick" and defines the most junior category in the kids' football academy)

There aren't many things that leave such a trace and a memory that you can still feel exactly the same way 41 years later. And if the case, it's unusual that something beyond those memories that are inextricably linked to your family, friends, or school can leave such a lasting mark when you're so young.

But some moments just stay with you. Forever.

It was the first day of training in the kids' academy. Looking back now it was a wonderful place to start, but in my childhood memories it was already an achievement and it was a source of pride – I had made it. Just two years later, aged 8, I had loftier goals of winning the World Cup with Italy and ideally as captain, as you're the first one to get your hands on the trophy. Luckily kids change their goals very quickly indeed. The magic of unconsciousness that gifts kids with the greatness of the dream. When we recall and recover that unconsciousness and that attitude for dreaming, we make special things happen.

Essentially the first day at a football club, the Bologna academy, was my first goal and that day I would achieve it.

It was my day.

We met up in "La Barca," an area of Bologna to the north-west of the city, which was home to a training ground where you start facing the green moving into the Po Valley. The training ground was massive and right at the other end of the facility, across the motorway, there was Casteldebole, the training home of the first team, the real players, the pros, the stars of "90° minute" and of the "Panini" sticker albums.

Between the "Chicks" of the academy and the Panini sticker album pros there was but a motorway you had to cross.

It didn't seem light years away.

Anything was possible.

It was the middle of the afternoon in early September when my dad took me to training, which in itself was unusual because he was normally working all day. What's more it was a very weird time and my father was working so hard. Just a few weeks earlier he had spent 3 days straight at the hospital, working day and night without ever coming home. I didn't understand why and I was constantly asking after him. I was told that the hospital needed all hands-on deck because it was "very full" at that time and that he, as a surgeon, could pitch in and help out all his colleagues. A little while later they gave that event a name and it was a new word to me. They told me it was a "massacre" and it had occurred in a place where lots of people all came together to catch the train. Sometime later I learned that essentially, for reasons unknown and unfathomable to everyone let alone a child of six, someone had decided to destroy 85 families.

In one go.

Using a bomb.

Lots of children would never see their mothers or fathers again, or even both. They would never play together again; they would never climb into their parents' bed for cuddles on a Sunday morning. Lots of parents would never again see their children. They would never hold their hands on a Sunday stroll to the park.

Just like that.

Wiped out.

Forever.

Not just for three days, which felt endless to me.

With no chance to say goodbye.

Without a word.

Without a hug.

That day though, at the start of September, a month after those tragic events, I, along with a group of around 30 kids, joined the Bologna youth academy. I would always remember it as one of the best days of my life.

And my dad took me, holding my hand.

I did likewise with my own son 37 years later, taking him to his first football team meet-up. I don't think he remembers much about it, but you never know whether something might stick.

It was nice day and I don't remember it being either hot nor cold. I don't think any external factors could distract me from the excitement of becoming a "Chick".

The car park opened onto a long tree-lined avenue and I can remember every step of the way. Away to my right someone was playing on a grass pitch with a sort of bent stick. So, the only real question that came to mind was, "Why is there no ball? A grass pitch, lots of kids. Where's the ball?"

That sure was a strange way to train towards winning the World Cup.

At the end of the avenue there was an old stone building with doors like gates, all evenly spaced, and windows too small to belong to a house. Away to the far left you caught sight of one, no hang on, two gorgeous massive football pitches. Maybe even three.

I was already in my kit. I don't think there's ever been a more pristine child in the world than I was that day. I was wearing the full kit they had provided, boots and all.

The white shirt with red and blue hoops on the upper part of the chest was tucked into my shorts so meticulously that perhaps only Sister Ignazia, my teacher, the strictest of the nuns at my primary school, would have been able to reproduce it.

The shorts were blue, and they sat just above the knee of my two spindly legs, which had however already graced the concrete of Piazza Trento Trieste, the greatest stage throughout primary school. The venue for some unforgettable matches against the school classes.

We wore two pairs of socks: Long white tights around the feet and blue football gaiters over the top. I used to like pulling up the under-sock and then turning it down over the gaiters to give it a different colour trim just below the knee. The boots, which came with the kit, were made by Tepa Sport. I thought they were the best boots in the world because we were the Bologna "Chicks" and only the best would do for us.

In truth, besides how they looked - which was very questionable - they didn't last long, and I soon fell in love with the boots I would go on to wear forever: adidas World Cup, for softer or damp pitches which required six studs. Or I'd switch to my adidas Copa Mundial with 13 moulded studs for firmer surfaces.

I only betrayed adidas twice in 35 years.

I once wore a pair of Patricks because they were the boots Michel Platini played with. I wanted to see if they'd help me hit pinpoint 60-yard passes.

I once bought a pair of Nikes because they were a brand-new make and they looked really cool.

This doesn't count but there was also the time when I bought a pair of Lotto, not to wear them but to remove the fluorescent green logo so I could sew it onto my World Cup in place of the three stripes. That's because during that period Giuseppe Giannini, my hero once I became a central midfielder, had that logo on his boots. But I didn't want to give up my adidas boots.

And I don't think "The Prince" – Giannini's nickname – wanted to either because I could recognise his boots from the sole, with their white lining and the three red stripes across the front of the foot. So, I wouldn't be fooled by the branding on the side, whatever it was.

Swapping the branding on the side of the boot by sewing another logo over the top was a tricky task. That task fell to an incredible old man who owned a cobbler shop right at the start of Via Azzurra, just a few yards from the back entrance to what would later become my high school. He was the best. The football boot guru of Bologna. Professional players went to his shop and he'd prepare their boots in the lead-up to their matches.

It was a lovely day and that was the day I met Maxi and Ricki, in that group of "chicks." I remember that kid, full of curls, Ricki, a bit shy, but already in love with the ball. They put us in couples to play and we were together. I don't remember Maxi with that level of detail, but I have this flash of a kid, who was looking a little bit smaller than me and had a smile as big as the sun.

That day, Maxi, Ricki, and I became "Pulcini" for Bologna.

The first training session was unforgettable.

They gave us some balls and we simply had to pass them to one another. Easy. I was good at it; I knew how to pass the ball and I committed to every pass as if it were the most inch-perfect assist of my life.

I will never forget a middle-aged man, who seemed old to me, but then again so did everyone over the age of 20. It looked like he was the head coach. And despite his age, he too was wearing football shorts and boots.

He was the most bow-legged person I had seen up until that point. When he put his feet together, his knees were so far apart that I might have even fit between them. I definitely would have done had I lay on my side.

We were split into groups and he moved from one group to the next. When he got to ours, he watched us for a bit. Then he told us to stop and leave the balls for a moment.

He asked us to lie down and roll around in the grass. I did so immediately because of course this exercise was no doubt key to winning the World Cup a few years later. We rolled around and then we lay face down on the ground. When he was face down, he asked us to look at the grass, then to close our eyes, to breathe it in and smell it.

He did it with us.

I can still remember the smell.

And I smelled it for 20 years in every training session and every match. Even when there was dew on the ground.

The small of the grass stays with us. Especially when it's been freshly cut.

It immediately takes me back – I can't help it.

Over time I developed the habit of only lacing up my boots when I got to the pitch, first on one knee and then on the other, after that fleeting moment when I could breathe in the scent of the grass.

If I have to play on it, I need to get to know the surface - the grass must be my friend.

That old man, who would later teach me to do keepy-ups with both feet, to control the ball in 10 different ways, and so many other great things, for our first lesson showed us what it means for a "Pulcino" to "stay in the pitch" and be in the game. By smelling the grass.

These days how you approach the game or "stay in the game" is all about how you set up tactically.

Setting up for a "Pulcino" means lying on the grass, gazing at it, embracing it and stepping into a world you'll never again leave behind. You will always be a part of that grass, so you best recognise it and learn to love it.

My father had already seen that old man. He'd recognised him too. He would later tell me that he was someone from Bologna who had dedicated his life to the football club – and Bologna alone. He had made more than 300 appearances in Serie A and scored nearly 100 goals.

He wore number 7, the right winger.

That would be my first number.

That would be my first position as a "Pulcino." My first way in the game.

PLAYING FOREVER

Opposite my house in Bologna stood Sant'Orsola hospital, the biggest one in the city and one of the leading facilities in the whole of Italy, with lots of people travelling from the south of the country to treat various conditions.

My father and Maxi's dad both worked there and we both lived opposite one of one of the entrances, next to the hospital's biggest car park.

The hospital was one big facility made up of lots of individual buildings, which housed doctors specialising in all sorts of things: doctors who would give you X-rays; those who treated tummy aches; others who dealt with headaches and so on and so forth. For each of the treatment there were different types of doctors, in different buildings.

That didn't seem like the most efficient way of doing things, but I wasn't really that fussed because my dad had been very clear with me. "Don't become a doctor," he'd said. When I was a child, I accepted that instruction without complaint, but I never really understood what he meant. When I went to see him at the hospital, he would be wearing a lovely long white coat and he looked really important and highly thought of, so that everyone was calling him "Professor." More importantly in my view he was dedicating all his time to take care of people and make them feel better and I thought that it was a great thing.

My mum was also a doctor and worked for many years in the same hospital, where they first met. Then she decided to dedicate her profession to take care of the kids in the schools of Bologna.

We were well off, we didn't want for anything and so I thought you could support a family well as a doctor. At Christmas we were used to receiving so many baskets with lot of food inside and I was especially happy about the ones with lots of chocolates.

Of course, it was hard work because he would come home at 8pm, just before I went to bed and sometimes he would have to stay in the hospital and work through the night or all-day Saturday and Sunday. My grandad was also a doctor, so was my uncle and my cousin was studying to become one. So, it seemed obvious that I too should become one.

But once my dad told me that being a doctor wasn't the problem with being a doctor. The issue was that in the hospital, decisions over who would do what and who would be given greater responsibility came down to "Politics" (which in Italy literally is a female name), who I assumed was the name of a very powerful lady because if you knew her you would go farther than others even if they were a better doctor than you.

At that time, I never worked out who Mrs "Politics" was, but I instinctively thought she was as stupid as a football coach who picks a bad player instead of a good one. And maybe even lose the game. For reasons that weren't rationally explainable. I thought that was unacceptable, so from a young age I decided that my dad was right and

I was better off not becoming a doctor because I didn't like the idea of losing matches when someone picked bad players maybe just because they knew them better.

A few years later I started to understand more. I remember one time when my dad had to sit a series of exams called a "concorso" to have even more responsibility at the hospital and I remember that as well as working he also studied so hard.

Then something unexpected happened: a few days before the exam he got a phone call telling him not to attend. It was like an order he had to follow.

I remember that he had several rows with my mum and I didn't understand exactly what was going on. But one thing was very clear back then even though I was really young: my mum never thought intimidation, hurdles or threats were a good enough reason to back down. That's how she was. She was brave, determined and persistent to the extreme. On that occasion she convinced my dad to keep going and to show who he was, even if it meant going against everything and everyone. She never gave up. And my dad went with her.

He went and he was obviously very good because he won the competition. In spite of everything. In spite of everyone.

I dunno. I think you should always pick the best players and always play to win. Mr or Mrs "Politics" wouldn't have made good football coaches.

Either way, between my house, Maxi's place and the hospital there was a patch of grass and a few trees. That was where Maxi and I used to spend whole afternoons when we didn't have training.

Most of the time it was just us.

I remember there were two trees with broad trunks and very high branches which didn't get in our way. The trees were right at the edge of the grass and just the right distance from one another as to make two goalposts. We judged the height of the bar with the naked eye.

We would take turns going in goal. One of us would take shots and the other would try to save them.

Thousands of times.

Endlessly.

That was until it got dark and they came to call us inside because it was already dinner time and obviously we hadn't done our homework. We were filthy and as usual we hadn't done anything.

Yet for us we had done the only thing that mattered. The only thing we needed to do. The only thing that made sense: playing football like there was no tomorrow.

Sometimes it poured it down with rain, other times it had been raining and we were up to our ankles in mud. And then there was the snow. Nothing stopped us. But the worst was when it was really dry because football shorts were really short back then, so you used to graze the side of your thighs by diving around in goal and it would take ages to heal. It was even worse when the wound stuck to your jeans. Brutally painful.

I really liked shooting for the far top corner. I must've practised that curler millions of times. I liked seeing the ball almost go level with the goal before darting into the corner while I was still wrapping my leg around the follow-through. Obviously, we used to try scoring straight from a corner. And with the outside of the boot, like Eder, the famous Brazilian wing of the 80's. At that time Roberto Carlos and Cafu were still kids, like us.

One year I tried to come up with a new way of striking the ball, "I will need it in the final of the World Cup...." I thought. Luckily consciousness and shame are not things that touch 10 year-old kids, freeing up imagination and courage.

Basically, I struck it with the laces but without bending my standing leg, so I didn't cut underneath the ball. But I wouldn't strike the middle of the ball but to one side of it to get it curling and put some spin on it. You had to do all that with your laces, which wasn't easy. My theory was to combine the power of hitting it with my laces with the spin from cutting across it. The concept was very similar to the three-toe technique – the one used by Roberto Carlos – except with the inside of the laces rather than the outside of the boot.

I remember that I worked on that technique for entire days and weeks, throughout the summer at my grandma's place in the countryside. A man who knew how to build things had made me a wooden goal on the lawn and I was spending days on end trying to take free-kicks and stacking chairs from the house to create a makeshift wall. I broke loads of them.

I would send the ball out a yard wide of the wall, the pile of chairs, before curling it back round the wall. It was a lovely strike but very hard to control.

In a friendly match during a pre-season training camp in the mountains (at the time of the under 12s) I took a free kick like that was only about 5-10 yards outside the box from a central position. I produced a wonderfully struck curler which clattered against the crossbar. It was hit so hard the ball rebounded back to where I had struck it from, just outside the D. It bounced up and I struck it first time with my laces. It hit the bar again and rebounded back to me once more. I couldn't believe it, but I felt a bit angry that the ball just didn't want to go in. I was insulted. So, I hit it again and once more it struck the bar but this time it spun back over the line. Three crossbars in a row, all struck first time. Unbelievable. I had never seen anything like it. It was the first friendly match of pre-season in the mountains at the end of the summer of 1986.

Now, here's the point: let's be honest, it was all looking incredible but also very much useless. It would have been way better to score with a rough strike, because the good ones they score, they don't hit 3 crossbars in a row. Not even if someone would count the points, there aren't credit points in football. Some things get clearer over time. Some years later, in the workplace it would become way more obvious that at the end of the game only results count. Yes, better if with style. Better if with replicable method and processes. Even more important, better with a strong organization development and with the best motivation and self-realization of all individuals that are part of the team or company. All critical factors that will add value and will give dimension to the results. But sometimes it's difficult to understand what comes first, because when you win and when you get results, everything else comes easier. Today, I wouldn't be able to say what's right or wrong, but I have no doubts that, like it or not, results are worthwhile, the rest it's all on top. Losing but playing well could gratify and justify or motivate in the very short term, as well as develop ideas, methods, organizations, strategies, plans, and processes that are perfect. But at the end you need to score, you need to win. Results count. That fourth launch of the Falcon 1 from Elon Musk's space X, that finally was successful in September 2008, as the first private rocket to reach orbit after 3 blown rockets, even the company was almost bankrupt, it made the whole difference.

Sometimes several of us played on the pitch at Sant'Orsola. My older brother would join us, as would two or three older friends who all lived in our block of flats. That would lead to some really hard-fought, brutal games and there was a real edge to them. It was 1986, a World Cup year, the one in Mexico, and every match was live or die because we would recreate Italy's games. I remember that we used to like playing Maxi and I against everyone else.

My brother's friends called me "Albar of Mexico." Because obviously it was my World Cup.

Maxi and I were the youngest there. But we'd still win.

Unless they kicked us off the park. Not even Gentile would scythe down Zico like that.

Maxi and I spent hours shooting, taking turns in goal, crossing and passing. If I wasn't on the field of Sant'Orsola I was at my place in the countryside where on some summer days, we would play football for up to 12 hours straight. I couldn't sleep at night because I kept thinking about kicking the ball. I would dream and wake up, over and over again, as if everything we did had started a record off that kept spinning and spinning without ever coming to a stop. I was delirious. I played football in my mind all night long.

The next morning my grandma would make us breakfast. We'd barely finished swallowing and we'd be outside again kicking the ball around.

That pitch in front Sant'Orsola hospital is no longer there.

A few years later they decided to build an underground car park. I'm sure it serves a purpose but from time to time I think about what the kids living in those apartment blocks are missing out on. Most of them are the children of my peers.

The truth is technology and innovation have provided the new generations with cutting-edge devices. The most prestigious innovation we had was our adidas "Azteca" ball, which was amazing when you hit it with curl. You could generate a lot more bend on it than you could with the "Tango," and it was a lot less heavy than the Tango when wet. They were the real issues that were solved by technology.

The issue technology sorted for us was the sponge ball that was crucial for playing with around the house, to limit the damage to objects and people. These days there are more screens than ever but we're losing playing fields. Or we watch fields on a screen rather than rolling around on them. In fact, our children no longer play video games, but they watch other people playing them while they talk at random.

I once asked my son, who is 10, why he did that? What was so interesting about watching other people computer games, instead of play rather himself? He answered, "Dad you also watch other people play football instead of playing yourself." I wanted to tell him that I was 47 and had 5 surgeries on my knees, but I didn't want to come across as defensive.

I chose to interrupt him instead and told him to come and play football with me in the park. Thankfully he can't yet say no to that.

FIRST MATCH

I can remember everything about my first match. And it's not that hard because there's very little to tell, in that I never got a kick. Or barely.

But let's start from the beginning.

I made my debut as a Bologna "Pulcino" one Saturday afternoon on a clay pitch full of stones on the eastern edge of the city, heading towards the coast. The pitch was called "Ca' Bassa" and was located on a tiny road just off Via Emilia between Idice and Ozzano.

I turned up to the ground with my dad. We parked just off the main road, but we couldn't see the pitch because it was sunken into the ground and surrounded by natural stands of grass and soil. It was dug out like the Santiago Bernabeu. Identical.

It was a 7-a-side pitch.

I wore number 7 - right wing.

I remember thinking that I had no idea where to go or where to run. Every time I moved the ball went in the other direction. And then when I went after the ball it shot away.

So, I held my position and it never came my way.

Life is really hard as a Pulcino because you're desperate to do well, but you've got no idea what to do.

My dad was there, and I had the chance to show him how good I was and that the next logical step in my football career would be a call-up to the national team. I'm sure I struck the ball at least once towards the opposition half, but that was it.

It was a tough start that didn't warrant a mark out of 10 but I was happy.

I'm almost certain that my dad, once we got home, told my mum that I'd played brilliantly. I think he said that every time, every Sunday, for every match, regardless of the score line, whatever position and whatever category I played.

My dad understood football and he had played to a good standard – you could tell as much when we played together. He controlled the ball well and he had a sensational half-volley. But he wasn't exactly objective when it came to me. In fact, he was anything but. And not only when I was a Pulcino either, but at every age group I played for. I remember I used to go to see him in the clinic and I'd run into his colleagues who would say, "You must be the footballer," which showed how my father saw me, how he judged my performances and how he described me to his colleagues.

I would smile shyly in response and my hundreds of freckles would all blend into one and almost become a pinky-red mask.

It was only later that I realised what all this meant to him. I grasp what goes on around me with logic and rationale but, when I watched my son play, I finally got what years of logic will never tell you and what any form of reason could never explain to me and will never be able to describe.

Logic and reason will never explain that which has no logic and goes beyond reason.

Because when you watch him play, you're with him every step of the way and with every kick of the ball. You watch him kick the ball while reliving moves you've already seen and predicting every movement and every possible solution.

And boy does Mattia strike the ball well. Clean. Firm. True. You can hear it from the sound it makes even before seeing the ball fly.

Sure, at 10 years old he still needs to deep dive the meaning of football, which isn't only about striking the ball and scoring. Something that works pretty well for him even when kicking from just after the midfield line.

But also moving, running, and making sacrifices.

Suffering.

And believe that it's never enough, as it would always be the very first day.

This is what the best players, and more in general all the champions in all sports, can do really well. They don't have only talent, but also the mental strength that drives and pushes them to go one yard more, one push up more, one lap more, one training session more, one sprint more, one free kick or one penalty training more. And there is never a moment when you say "done" or "that's enough," but it's always like the first day. An attitude and a mentality that you can find clearly also in successful professionals, or in the best entrepreneurs. When studying it's pretty much the same thing.

I am not sure if "Matti" will become a footballer, but every time that I can see him playing in the pitch, to me that's the most important final in football history and anyway, to me he is my footballer and in my universe, he is the number 1.

It's also a shame that I truly understood what linked me, football and my father once it was too late. But there are some things you only understand when the shoe is on the other foot, when you change ends and when the match is turned on its head.

In the second half of my match, watching my son play and watching the grace of his football, I relived a bond with my father that I've never been able to recognize, understand and love.

Over time, the memories of that first game have faded to such an extent that I'm simply left with the feeling of striking the ball and a reminder of equal parts eagerness and confusion.

Years later on the first day of high school, I ended up sitting next to a really nice, curly-haired guy who became one of my best friends at school. The first time I went to his house, we took the bus towards Ozzano. We got off along the Via Emilia, turned right and there we were in Via Ca' Bassa, facing the Ca' Bassa pitch, scene of my first ever match when I hadn't got near the ball.

I hadn't ever been back since then. But I hadn't forgotten it.

I've just checked on Google Maps and the pitch is no longer there.

It's been swallowed up by a warehouse on one side and a row of terraced houses on the other.

That's not the only memory that has been buried unfortunately.

But some memories as well as some pitches will always stay with you. Just like how some people never really leave you.

Some of that will remain.

And you begin to wonder, ultimately, what's left of football?

WORLD CUP '82

In 2018 my son was eight years old, the same age I was in 1982.

I was very lucky to be eight in 1982 and watch all of the World Cup games with my dad.

And I had high hopes for the 2018 World Cup because the roles would be reversed. I, now a father, and my eight-year-old son with me. Same age, a World Cup, together.

I wanted to see history repeat itself and cement my passion for football so I could pass it down to my son.

Indeed, I can remember everything about that World Cup in 1982. Me, my father, football, the heroes, the triumph, the celebrations, the colours.

Unfortunately, my son won't remember anything because Italy didn't even qualify. That was down to the incompetence of those running the Italian game, the arrogance of a wrong coach and a missing a crop of young players after the generation of Francesco Totti, Alessandro Del Piero, Daniele De Rossi, Andrea Pirlo and Fabio Cannavaro.

There was nothing after them.

The only consolation was being able to cheer on Switzerland, our second nationality, on their run to the round of 16. We even bought four shirts, one for each of the family.

1982 was for me the best World Cup ever.

Let's be careful, though – 2006 had a few of the greatest talents of our football, players of such unique class and unmatchable talent as Totti, Del Piero, Pirlo, De Rossi, Inzaghi, Cannavaro, together with all other world champions. In Geneva, the block where we were living still remembered us well, the 20 Italian friends watching the games at our place. But when you are 32 years old, the level of consciousness limits the imagination and doesn't build the myth.

So, in 1982, I was 8 years old, which is an age in between the dream and the reality and when characters quickly become heroes.

Football-wise it was the start of the modern game, where you began to consistently see the tactics, cohesion and togetherness of a team. Where fitness levels were already visible but where individual talent and technique could still win matches. I would say the same about 1986 and 1990, but then I think tactics took over and the physical preparation and the tactics partially replaced the genuine technical abilities or at least diluted them. And let's exclude for now Del Piero, Totti, Pirlo as well as Baggio who were, are and will always be completely off the chart.

I think the same about Formula 1, where technology was of course important until the early 1990s, but individual drivers could still win races on their own, leading to some legendary rivalries: Alain Prost; Ayrton Senna; Nigel Mansell; Nelson Piquet. Great cars, but great drivers behind the wheel. So that the courage and the big heart were creating the myth.

I've always liked the human stories in football, the heroes of the game. They were imperfect, but so generous to make any other weakness a marginal sin. They were giving it all for the game, for the fans, but specially for their team.

Not for statistics or for the next contract.

And not for one more social post.

But because in those 90 minutes, and in that 100x50mt space, it was the right time and the right place in which everything had a meaning, maybe their entire life.

So, in my childish imagination '78, '82, '86 and even '90 were the years of heroes.

I remember Mario Kempes with his power, his skill and the way he stole the march on defenders. Or how about Osvaldo Ardiles and his ability to get to the by-line? People like Oleg Blokhin, the Russian striker, or Grzegorz Lato the bald Polish midfielder, who along with Zbigniew Boniek led Poland to their best ever finish, when they only lost to the future world champions.

The Brazil side of Zico, Falcao and Eder, who used to shoot directly from the corner. He was arguably the best player to ever strike the ball with the outside of his boot. Until Roberto Carlos surpassed him many years later, writing the three-toe technique into the pages of football history. Or until Cafu reinvented the right back, combining dynamism, running, and unique skills, becoming at the same time both right back and right forward. No one can forget the 3 consecutive sombreros he did to Pavel Nedved.

Perhaps that Brazil team didn't achieve what it should have done, but it was arguably the greatest team ever.

Men and heroes.

So were the German side of Manfred Kaltz, Bernd Schuster, Paul Breitner, Hansi Muller, Uli Stielike, Karl-Heinz Rummenigge and Pierre Litbarski. The victory against that Germany team still feels unbelievable. The Cameroon team of Thomas N'Kono and Roger Milla, the Argentina of Daniel Passarella, Daniel Bertoni and Jorge Valdano. Belgium with Jan Ceulemans. Peter Shilton and Kevin Keegan of England. France had a midfield of Alain Giresse, Jean Tigana, Luis Fernandez and Michel Platini, named "les carré magique." Spain had Luis Arconada.

All teams full of heroes, very few of them great athletes and none of them were soldiers carefully following a tactical plan. They were players with passion, skill, imagination, ingenuity and power.

And heart.

They wore their hearts on their sleeves.

I wouldn't know if they carried out the job the coach asked of them. But they were top players. I think of Platini, who would hit 60-yard balls over the top and put strikers through on goal. Every time. I don't think that was a training ground routine, but it was definitely the technical skill and vision that only Francesco Totti at his peak could rival: a player who prompted this infamous line from Zdenek Zeman the first time he watched him, "This kid has eyes in the back of his head."

I don't mean to disparage or play down the very valuable role the likes of Arrigo Sacchi, Johan Cruyff and Pep Guardiola played in revolutionising the game after the 90s and I'd put Zeman in that category too. Because you only need to watch their teams play for 10 minutes and you know who the coach is. They invented methods, patterns, moves, movements and timings that made football even more competitive and spectacular. But it was also more tactical and physical and that had an impact on the players' individual development, once physical attributes and the ability to function with a formation became key.

Diego Maradona, who I number among the heroes, made every team he played for great at national, continental and global level. Teams that would not have been at that level without him. Not only Napoli but also Argentina in 1986, a team that on paper was much weaker than the '78 and '82 sides.

My sticker album of all of those heroes that I spent hours collecting, swapping, finding, sticking and studying. I knew them all. Off by heart. A Panini sticker album was a real commitment, you had to sweat it, but it gave you some unforgettable memories, certainly a lot more than Google. Plus, when things are easily accessible and you don't have to work hard enough to get them they are also less memorable and definitively less mythical. Please try and explain that to my children and to all their friends, all born in a world where everything responds to the command of just a finger.

You had to work hard to complete a Panini sticker album and it became a celebration of my heroes.

And I had to be one of them.

So, when I was eight years old, I decided that I would play for Italy, looking at the calendar, give or take... yes, at the 1994 World Cup, or, latest, at the 1998 one.

Maxi and Ricki would be there with me, I was certain.

Decision taken.

That World Cup in 1982 brought me closer to a world which was much bigger than simply being a "Pulcino for Bologna FC." The national anthem, and your colours that tell you where you belong and separate you from all the others. It was a new world for me.

The concept of a national team was also new to me i.e., seeing players that would normally line up against one another every week come together to play for the same team. It seemed a bit weird at first. Why would they kick lumps out of each other one day, then be happy to play for the same team the next?

But as soon as the national anthem was over you understood why.

It wasn't only a game that was on the line but the pride of a nation, a shirt, a flag that brought everyone together and that everyone identified with: they were the Azzurri. For a child of eight this was a whole new discovery.

I remember asking my father why they wore blue and not white, red and green. In our opening games we played Cameroon, Poland and Peru and their shirts were almost identical to or at least portrayed the colours of their flags. The same was true when we faced Brazil and Argentina or Poland again and Germany.

I never understood the answer. It dated back to people and events that I didn't know and a time before the flag was created. Apparently blue represents the colours of Italy (or something similar to Italy) before the tricolour flag was created.

But the kits changed every year or so. So why could they not design a new set of Italian shirts after the day in which they decided the colours would be white, red and green?

Either way I liked the "Azzurro" ("light blue" in Italian, to not confuse with the "les blue" of the French team please).

My favourite player was Bruno Conti because he played my position. That was how I saw things. He played my position, not the other way around.

He was very good to the extent that he was voted player of the tournament. He was the most "Brazilian" player among all our players. He was quick, skillful, intelligent and he always did a trick where he'd shift the ball back quickly with his heel and change direction. Obviously, my sponge ball and the corridors of my house were perfect to hone the skill that would become one of my favourite tricks.

Bruno Conti won the World Cup with Italy in 1982.

A year later he won the league with Roma.

A year after that in 1984, when I was 10, he put his penalty shot over the crossbar in the Champions League final against Liverpool. From that day on, I'll always be a Roma fan.

I was once having dinner with a Juventus fan who I didn't know that well, and he said to me, "How can you Roma fans support a team that never wins anything?" I hadn't actually asked myself that question in that exact way... but it was pretty obvious to me that winning had never been a factor when it came to choosing my team. Plus, everyone knows that Roma fans are chosen, not the other way around. But for some reason, hearing someone ask me that reminded me what "unconditional passion" is all about. It's not tied to any factor that decides things for you. I remember replying "I don't know exactly why but as you said it's not because the team win... so I love Roma unconditionally. Roma chose me, the club chose me. How about you?" He mumbled something.

It's interesting as football can reveal some truths of human nature, like unconditional love, that are very rare to see in action.

Coming back to the World Cup: it was a triumph.

I had no idea what a victory like that meant. During the final my father and I couldn't tear ourselves away from the TV. It was very late for me, but it was an exception to my very strict 8:30 bedtime. That meant it really was unusually important.

We didn't celebrate Paolo Rossi's goal as much as we should have, because in some games breaking the deadlock can almost be a disadvantage, especially if you're not the stronger side. My father thought that too when Antonio Cabrini missed a penalty in the first half. He was furious when it happened but then he said, "Well maybe it's better off that way because they're really good and you would have kept us pinned back in our own half for 60 minutes."

He couldn't prove his theory, but it seemed plausible.

Then 30 yards from goal Bruno Conti did that piece of skill that I loved with his heel, quickly changing direction. Then the ball went out to the right and was crossed in for Marco Tardelli, who on the stretch struck the ball so powerfully with his laces that you almost didn't see it leave his boot. But you could clearly see the net bulge behind Toni Schumacher.

Tardelli's scream is one of the most iconic moments in Italian football history. When you're eight, you love football, you're with your dad, you watch a World Cup final, you're Italian and you see Tardelli run away screaming, you've witnessed something you'll never forget.

Then Conti ran down the wing, played the ball to Alessandro Altobelli who controlled it, shifted it and fired it into the back of the net before two defenders could get to him.

A triumph.

Despite how late it was, we went out into the street. I felt like my father was delighted to be able to share that moment with me. He didn't say much and he wasn't very emotional - in the sense that he never abandoned himself to too many emotions - but he held my hand as we walked to Via Mazzini, the biggest road in our neighbourhood, where there was a stream of people, cars and flags that lit up the night sky.

As he held my hand, we watched how people expressed joy.

It was our joy and it was everyone else's. It was loud and colourful.

It was football that gives you this energy that you can't explain, and you can't understand unless you're a part of it.

We were world champions.

My father was happy.

I had made a decision.

I told to myself: one day, dad, I'll be the one giving you that joy.

THE UNBEATABLES

The "Esordienti" age group at the Bologna academy.

We were an unbeatable team.

I had never seen an unbeatable team, it's on the nature and on the round-shape of the ball. There aren't edges. There aren't absolutes.

It's the real beauty of the game. The ball is rounded, an assurance of equality at kick-off and everything and anything can happen till the very end. Nothing is a given.

So much so that there are some wonderful fairy tales that upset the established order like Verona under Osvaldo Bagnoli and Claudio Ranieri's Leicester side - teams that overturned the odds and brought unexpected joy to those who humbly, proudly and patiently deserved it.

So I had never truly seen an unbeatable team in my life.

Yet we were.

Maxi, Ricki and I, plus another 15 12-year-olds. We were.

Our team was. It was the unbeatable team.

The "Esordienti" (under 12 years old) championship is exciting because you start to play proper football. When you're a "Pulcino" you just roll around with the ball and on the ball. And the ball follows you more than you follow it. Basically... you roll around.

Like the "Chicks," by name and by nature.

Whereas as an "Esordiente" you start to play triangles, cross the ball onto the head of a teammate (or at least you try), counterattack, cover, spread the play, slow and quicken the tempo. You also begin to shoot from outside the box and try to hit free kicks over the wall and into the top corner to blow away the cobwebs. You try many times and you don't really blow away many cobwebs, but occasionally you really do.

Then you realise that if you target right below the cross bar, the keeper will never get there. That was a great "bazza" as we say in Bologna - a trick. There was a 15-inch window all across the top that would guarantee you a goal nine times out of ten because as an "Esordiente" the goals are big, but the keepers aren't yet. That was the trick.

We didn't have any superstars in our team, but we were all really good at doing exactly what we were supposed to.

The goalkeeper, Lorenzetto, was solid between the sticks. I never saw him produce any wonder saves but on the odd time someone got a shot off, he was there to save it. He was, how to say, basic but effective.

Marione, the sweeper, despite a frame that suggested he enjoyed his tortellini a little too much, was exemplary. He was laid-back, neat and tidy on the ball and timed his challenges well. He would drop off, close down, double up or push everyone up with the timing and confidence of someone who had always done that job. He was never in a state of anxiety. I don't think I ever saw Marione short of breath. He never panicked.

Apart from that time when he kicked that ball exactly in the top corner... his one. Don't tell me about that cobweb. But it also happens to the very best, I saw it happening in 40 years of football.

Maxi was the most effective and efficient stopper I've ever seen play. Short (he was at that age... he'd eventually reach 6'1") but quick, tenacious and determined. He was unpredictable in the sense that especially when we were younger you never knew where his balls would end up, which was a mystery both to us and the opposition. But the only thing you did know was that he'd always get the ball. With his foot, his chest, head or backside. He always won the ball. I don't know if it was good timing, or he was jammy. Probably both.

He always got to the ball first and if he wasn't he would get there at the second or third attempt, but he always took the ball.

And you know what? If he didn't take the ball, then he'd take something else. I don't think the strikers liked it but that was just the way it was. Over the years he also caught a couple right on the nose.

I've always admired Maxi's focus and his ability to transform as he was entering the pitch. Calm outside the lines, a warrior inside the pitch. He could go 15 minutes without seeing the ball, but he would never lose sight of how far the striker was away from him. And when the ball came, he'd already beaten him to it. Always. Or almost. No one could match him for man-marking ability. A defender who always got at least 6.5-7/10, including eventual points subtracted. A perfect pick for Fantasy Football fans.

He would become another person on the pitch. Maxi was never a fighter or a troublemaker. He was your typical well-behaved, fairly relaxed kid. But when he stepped onto the football pitch, something changed, he really showed you who was boss. He was a warrior, that's what he turned into.

As for his ability with the ball? Maybe don't ask him to shoot. Especially if your car is parked behind the goal.

Maxi was, is and will always be a free spirit. While as a man-marker he would always find his reference point, the opponent, as a man he would always seek freedom of thought and expression.

Maldo bossed the midfield. Take Marione for his approach, shed a few points and add technical ability in passing and controlling the ball. A velvety stride, never in a fluster, he'd get the ball and keep it moving. And then he'd go and get it again. I really liked Maldo's style of play and a few years later when I started to operate as a playmaker, he stuck in my mind as someone to emulate. Assured, tidy and calm. He wasn't super quick. But that's where the two guys either side of him came in.

Vicki played on the right of the 3-man midfield. He was both a brilliant footballer and a brilliant athlete. He was one of the guys who would go the furthest in the game out of our crop, before he took up five-a-side and even became a coach. Vicki really was tough. He could win the ball back, start counterattacks and reset the tempo. He would get into shooting positions like few others, and he would always spot a teammate in space.

Ricki, who played to the left of the three, was a classy player who had skill, read the game well and was passionate about the Beautiful Game. He could pick out the strikers and make late runs into space. Quick and more attacking- than defensive-minded, he was also good at pulling wide to the cross the ball or cut inside from the flank. He read the game well, so he was able to both find teammates in the right space with a risky pass, but also pull into space to receive the ball. At that age playing without the ball was easier said than done.

He liked to strike the ball. I've always thought that Ricki took immense pride and joy in seeing a well-struck football. I think he always focused more on striking the ball well and providing assists than he did on scoring goals. Partly due to unselfishness, because Ricki was always a great team player, but also partly due to his love for flawless technique as opposed to the scoresheet.

He liked to dribble. But once again that wasn't out of him being selfish, which is typical of lots of technically gifted players. It was quite the opposite. He enjoyed the aesthetics of a nice move, of a piece of skill, of the game itself. It was never just for the sake of it or for personal reasons. He ran for himself and his teammates.

And he always celebrated the success of his teammates as much or more than what he was doing for himself. This is true in his game, as well as in his life.

Like all number 10s he would pick his head up to see the game. Very rarely to strike the ball.

Plus Ricki was such a fair player. I don't think I ever saw him get sent off throughout our entire time in the academy and 9 times out of 10 when he was booked it was for dissent.

Apart from that one time many years later. It was a very tense game, and he was taking a throw-in when an opponent just stood right in front of him. Furious he threw the ball straight at the guy's head from a yard away and hit him full in the face. He hurled himself to the ground. Some of us are still laughing about that one. I think Ricki spent the whole week of his suspension with a grin on his face.

The other guy wasn't laughing.

On the left, Ricci very nearly made it as a pro. If you think of a pacy left winger could change the tempo of a game, he's the guy who comes to mind. Small, quick, skillful. One of those players who move from zero to 10 in a second, he was past you before you could even move. Not many had his acceleration. He could cut inside and shoot or get to the by-line. He crossed the ball well and had he tracked back a bit more he could have given Ricki the chance to get a breather in.

The centre-forward was a goal scorer. Lots of goals. That was all he did and he got hatfulls. Ultimately that's the job of a striker - to score goals. He would rarely win an odd tackle, maybe 5 or 6 in a season, but he scored goals. Busso. He was powerfully built - maybe he was a bit heavy, but he wasn't really fat - he wasn't that quick, nor that skillful, nor that intense.

But he scored goals. I don't know, see if you can find fault with him.

I was the right winger. At that age I had the advantage of having two legs longer than 90% of the other players my age. I could control the ball fairly well and I could run like the wind. I could set off from the edge of my own box, play the ball in front of me, get to the by-line and cross it in. There was not really a lot of merit or talent in this, I just was faster than any other of my age group. But there was one other thing that I could do well, very well in fact. I could put the ball on a plate for my teammates. My crosses in the air were fairly famous, and I lost count of how many I put on Busso's head.

This could repeat more times during the same match, so, if you happened to be in the box, the ball would most likely hit you. That was pretty much how it was.

Then perhaps once I got to the opposition box rather than getting to the by-line I'd cut inside, most of the time having already gone past the entire defence. So, I'd get quite a few goals too.

When Ricki was on form that meant three assists and one free kick. If Ricci was on his game, he would beat four players every time he got the ball. Vicki would smash two in from outside the box. I would probably have delivered minimum 2 or 3 well-placed crosses for Busso to score.

That was how it was. All of our games were like that.

You might say it was easy. Well, it wasn't that easy because our coach also wanted us to pass the ball, to build moves, play triangles, make overlapping runs, push up as a unit and complete at least 10 passes before scoring a goal... all that jazz. We didn't think all that was so important.

The fact remains that we won them all. There was only one team that could compete with us - the guys from Borgo Panigale, who I believe were called "Borgo." It was tough when we played them because our winning margin would come down to two or three goals. I think there was one time where we had a really close shave and the game finished 4-2. I think that was the hardest match of the entire season.

What made things trickier was the fact that the pitch in Borgo Panigale was pretty small and so that increased the randomness of the game.

At full time, every other week when Bologna played at home, our parents would drop us off in the city centre and my teammates and I would grab a burger at Burghy before all jumping on a bus to see the first team play.

That was our Sunday, all together.

There was nothing else I wanted in life: Maxi, Ricki, me, our team.

An unbeatable Sunday. An unbeatable team.

As luck would have it that year, while we were beating all comers, Bologna also had an incredible side. Their style was dubbed "champagne football" thanks to a new coach called Gigi Maifredi. Many years later I discovered another coach who could inspire the same emotions. He was from the Czech Republic.

To be honest I always thought that Bologna won because we were there watching. Because we were unbeatable and so Bologna would be too.

I always wondered where the real strength of our side lay. And every time I came back to the same memories: every week I couldn't wait to go to training or a match with our team, my friends. That's because I loved football and that training session would change the entire complexion of the day. It's like on your first day of holiday you plan to sleep in and yet you wake up and get up earlier than usual because you're so excited.

But what made everything very special was the fact that I was lucky enough to do what I loved most, with the people I most wanted to do it with - my best friends.

I wouldn't have wanted to play with anyone else in the world.

It was a true friendship, one that does away with any notion of internal or personal rivalry, and allows everyone at any time, whether they were a starter or not, to focus on three things: always help one another out, play for each other and win. We really liked one another and that went way beyond just simply being a team.

Football, Burghy, crisps and the stadium. That was everything to us.

I've never seen, felt or experienced anything else like it.

It was unbeatable.

We were unbeatable.

"ESORDIENTI" ON THE PITCH AND IN LIFE

(*)",,Esordienti" in the Italian Junior leagues is the under 12 age group

(**) "Giovanissimi" in the Italian Junior leagues is the under 14 age group

The three years including the last year of Esordienti* and 2 years of Giovanissimi** age groups, were a whole new adventure for all of us in the team. That was because it was the first time that our parents let us go out on our own. Or rather as a group.

Or, in fact, in a pack.

We started after the game. We used to play on Sunday mornings and once the match was over and we'd showered, our parents would take us into the city centre. They would drop us off at the end of Via Ugo Bassi, where we would all meet up and begin our time as teenagers on the streets of Bologna, on our own. We felt all grown up.

Back then Burghy was in Via Rizzoli directly opposite Palazzo Re Enzo. It was the most central point of the city centre. We would all eat hamburgers and chips and drink Coca-Cola or Fanta. There were always at least six or seven of us and sometimes as many as ten of us and we'd always make a bit of a racket when it came to our burping contests. Maxi and Cecco always used to win. Ricki and I would be mortified because we were the only ones with a sense of shame. We would feel so embarrassed. It all came to a head when they were started to throw chips at trays on nearby tables especially if there were girls sitting there. Then they acted like nothing had happened, as if no one noticed.

Then it was off to the stadium.

We would take the bus that stopped right outside Burghy.

We would go into the stadium via the main stand because, as Bologna academy players, we had free season tickets. We liked to go at the top of the main stand, and it was a really fun season because we were in Serie B and we wiped the floor with everyone. Gigi Maifredi, who had taken charge that year, 1987, won the league with Bologna with a record-breaking promotion campaign, in his first season.

I remember that team as the most attacking side I had ever seen up until that point. That Bologna team were very similar to Zeman's Foggia or his Pescara side that won Serie B many years later. The following year Bologna stayed up in Serie A and the one after that they qualified for the UEFA Cup. They were three wonderful years.

They called it "Champagne football" because it was sparkling, quick and undoubtedly addictive but also because people claimed Gigi Maifredi was a big drinker. Maybe only Alberto Malesani, years later, was the only one who could beat him on that score.

There were some incredible players. The legendary Renato Villa played centre back. Small, stocky, even a bit clumsy and certainly not graceful on the ball, he was nonetheless very effective. He was a legend because somehow, in some unknown, miraculous way, he always came away with the ball. His blocks were memorable. When everyone else had lost hope and the opposition player was about to score – that's when he arrived. The legendary "mythical Villa."

Gianluca Luppi and Marco Antonio De Marchi were two classy, pacy, skillful full-backs. They both ended up joining Juventus.

Eraldo Pecci, who had played with Maradona and who was better than most at setting the tempo, ran the midfield. I remember when he ruptured his meniscus, he had surgery and was back out there exactly a week later. That tells you everything about the spirit of that era and the spirit of those players.

He was supported in midfield by Paolo Stringara and Giancarlo Marocchi, who came through the Bologna youth teams and made his debut in Serie B aged 17. After securing promotion with Bologna in 1988, Marocchi joined Juventus and won a league title, the Coppa Italia twice, the Super Cup, the Champions League and of course he was part of the team that finished third at Italia 90. He also scored more than 30 goals. There haven't been many midfielders as complete as him. I see him from time to time in Milano Marittima because he occasionally has lunch or dinner at the beach club I always go to.

The striker Lorenzo Marronaro was short and lightning quick. He would drift in from the left flank and scored bags of goals. He struck 21 in that record-breaking campaign, and he remains the last Bologna player to have won the "Capocannoniere" title (top scorer of the league) as the league's top scorer. Loris Pradella played alongside him at centre-forward and he also found the back of the net 10 times that season.

That was a wonderful Bologna side that played a very high line. They would squeeze up the pitch and press high with the backline just a few yards behind the halfway line. So, it was a very brave team too.

That year Arrigo Sacchi's Milan side were doing very well, with a very similar style of play built around pressing, resisting pace, minimizing space between the lines, a high defensive line and very quick forward passes. He also had the three Dutchman of course – Bologna didn't.

Once the game was over, all of us from the team took a nice walk back to the meeting point with our parents and then it was off home.

From the second year we even started to stay on for a third stop: after Burghy and the stadium... we went for a pizza in the evening.

This requires a bit more detail.

Typically, the line-up for the evening out was as follows: Albi, Maxi, Ricki, Cecco, Troccio, Marione, Vighe and Simo, plus some others who would join from time to time. There were two dreadful rituals we always did.

The first was to fill a glass with all of the most disgusting things imaginable. Like Coca-Cola, Fanta, chilli oil, slices of pizza, mozzarella and salt. Then someone had to down it in exchange for 10,000 Lira. I never did it and it still gives me chills just to think about, whereas others approached it with a lot more courage than me.

And then there were the burping contests. This is not something I'm particularly proud of and that's partly because I didn't have the talent for it.

That was Maxi and Cecco's domain.

Once there was a nasty incident. We were in a pizzeria in a side street off Via Indipendenza. I think it was called Via dei Falegnami and the pizzeria was named after it.

The entire pizzeria went completely silent for 10 long seconds because of something that was more like a scream than a burp.

I had time to think what would have happened had my parents found out. Everyone was staring at us. It was embarrassing. It was too ridiculous not to laugh like idiots, but too embarrassing to bear.

In those 10 seconds I learned all about shame.

That's when a waiter came by and kicked us out, while one of our guys asked if we could finish our pizzas first. They kicked us out on our ears.

To be fair, looking back, they were right to. But it's also true that when it comes to a group of ten 13-year-olds, out for the first time unaccompanied, you can't exactly expect them to show and tell a lecture of social etiquette

Either way, once we were outside the pizzeria, we started to ask one another. Had we really gone overboard, or was the red card not proportionate to the fault? To tell the truth that was probably our biggest offence as teenagers as far as I can remember. In the context of sport, friendship, a team, freedom and breaking the rules, it's alright to be fair. I fear that when our children will be the same age, we will have a lot more things to worry about.

Anyway, we never did go back to Pizzeria dei Falegnami – we were too embarrassed. We would keep acting up but never badly enough to be kicked out again. Let's just say we downsized our misbehaving and tried to rein in the troublemakers.

Game (ours), Burghy, game (Bologna), pizza.

The best Sundays of our lives.

COACHES, TEAMS AND ROLES

I've always admired coaches.

Not only because they're in charge and they decide who plays and who doesn't. And not only because they teach kids how to play football... so, as a kid, I always thought that they obviously needed to know how to play well.

Not only because they choose the system and the game plan, something which has always really intrigued me.

But above all because they have 18 children to work with and they have to get the most out of each and every single individual whilst simultaneously bringing all of these different components together to create one unit: a team.

There was something very special in the football and the teams of those times. Something that gets me thinking on how football is changed and how the role of the individual vs. the team is also changed. It was the integrity and indivisibility between the numbers on the shirt and the role you play in the team. Both were coming above the individual player.

Yes, think about the shirts' numbers: they were important because representative of the role in the team. The team and the role within the team were everything. The numbers were not representative of the individual, and they were not owned by the individual.

1 goalkeeper, 2 right back, 3 left back, 4 central midfielder, 5 and 6 centre back (6 sweeper in some tactics), 7 right wing, 8 and 10 right

and left midfielders, 9 striker, 11 left wing. With some adaptations depending on the tactics.

When the coach was calling the line-up, assigning the numbers, in the silence of the locker room, your heart was beating faster. Faster than when the teacher handed in the results of the last math test.

Today the number on the shirt is not any more representative of the role, but it represents the individual player. It even belongs to the individual player.

How football has changed...

The relevance of the players and their numbers was in the role they had to serve the team.

Not for themselves.

Some things, for me, change everything.

Anyway, in this scheme of team, based on roles, represented by numbers above and beyond any individual, the goal of the coach is to maximise the overall result while enhancing individual talents and contributions.

It sounds easy.

But it's not that easy.

Getting results as a team, playing as a unit versus the role of individuals has been and still is a significant subject of debate on organisation matters, and they are factors that highly correlate with culture and people's behaviours both in sport and work environments.

You hear about "teamwork" everywhere as the yardstick for harmony, cooperation and collaboration in the workplace. But sometimes these references to a "team" are taken out of context and lose their nature and their meaning, becoming a label. Sometimes empty.

I've observed, in some workplaces, three circumstances that drift away from the essence of teamwork.

The first is the confusion when applying individual accountability and team collaboration.

The second happens when there is a separation between accountability and decision making.

The third is about the "minimum common denominator", which implies flattening of the individual abilities in favour of team homogeneity or even to project an image of team unity.

Working as a team is about having a common goal, working with a shared strategy, and applying very precise roles and responsibilities.

Collaborating within the team connects the roles, but it doesn't change them.

Collaboration builds on a base of clear-cut roles and decision-making authority, not in their place. The shirt's number, the role, should be clear.

It is very important a highly collaborative environment but does not replace the clarity of roles and accountabilities (and hence decision making) unless in very exceptional circumstances, like when a striker comes back in the defensive line to cover for a defender who is badly and suddenly out of place.

When an over-drive of collaboration is needed, this is a symptom of some organizational outages. In this case, the use of collaboration, in place of a clear decision authority, creates the ambiguity typically linked "collective decisions" or "collective responsibilities". Those concepts are contradictions by themselves.

Very clear individual accountabilities and decisions are functional to the performance of the team (the striker attacks, the centre back defends, somebody takes the corner, somebody receives it, somebody takes the penalty...) to deliver the maximum collective result, via the best individual decisions and contribution.

When the referee blows for a penalty, only one player steps up to take it.

Not five players all together for team spirit or collaboration attitude.

And nor do five people decide who will take it.

And nor do five players practise taking penalties every training session to perfect their ability.

It's just one guy.

That's his job, his role, his task and we rely on him to get it done. That individual will stay on, after the end of the normal training to take fifty penalties and improve towards excellence. Sometimes under the rain and until the floodlights are turned off, while his teammates will be already having a nice hot shower.

And that's fine.

And if he scores, he scores for everyone.

But he shoots and he decides.

Goalkeepers mustn't go up for corners, but you rely on them when you're defending one and they come off their line shouting "Keeper's!"

On the corners in our favour, one goes to take it, the one that has that great curved kick, while other players go up in the box and use their head to hit the ball, jumping higher than all opponents. They have different skills, and probably different physical characteristics, and they will train differently during the week, who kicks and who goes for the header.

And if the one player scores with the headers, we all score. Who scored, who kicked the corner, all players on the pitch, all the ones on the bench, all the warehousemen. Everyone scores in that precise moment.

But let's be careful.

If the corner is not kicked right, who kicked is the one and only accountable. While who kicked it right and the teammate arrives in the box late, then who is late is the one and only accountable. Everyone sees it. There is transparency and everyone is aware.

And that's fine.

One scores, and scores for everyone.

Sometimes one makes a mistake, and all suffer the consequences.

It's visible. It's transparent.

It's acceptable and it's totally accepted in sport

It's the rule of the team game. There isn't any ambiguity. And there is a great sense of individual responsibility and collective impact.

Importantly, something not obvious, there is no shame in individual talents and exceptional individual performance when you play as a team. This is not in conflict with team play. Sometimes you may be needed to go solo, it's part of the game. It's part of the responsibilities of each role.

The second circumstance that could be observed is the split between decision making and accountability when the entity in charge of decision-making, is not the same having the accountability on the results – or the consequences – of the decision. It's like saying that the physiotherapist decides how and where who takes the penalty should kick it.

For some this is not a problem in a collaborative environment because "we are all a team" and we make it right or wrong all together.

Yes. Tell it to who takes the penalty.

Decisions and the consequences of those decisions cannot be separated. In the same way, decision making cannot be separated from accountability. When they are separated, the level of involvement and accuracy of the decision maker decreases, because who makes the decision will not be impacted by the outcome. And there will be a decrease in ownership of who is accountable for the results related with that decision, because didn't make that call.

The third situation is the case of the lowest common denominator, as a consequence of a strange interpretation of "playing as a team".

When you play the left winger through on goal and he's lightning quick - much quicker than all of us - we don't expect him to wait for the slower players before he shoots... so we score all together because we are a team. The quickest player mustn't wait for the slowest simply to give the impression that no one will be left behind, or because "we wouldn't look like a team."

That way, rather than having someone appear slower, we're all slower as a result. A slow team for the sake of looking like a team. Homogeneous, yes, but slower.

Instead, we need the fastest of us to run faster than anyone else, especially faster than all opponents.

When instead of maximizing individual talents, they get diluted in favour of team homogeneity, averaging in collective average, we create a minimum denominator that unifies everyone. A homogeneous team, yes, but average.

The team average doesn't move up the team in the overall league ranking.

If the striker scores, yes, it moves it.

It's fundamental that each and every one contributes at the very best of their own characteristics and talent, and not in the average of the team.

Youth-team coaches are well aware of their role - namely to put together a team by taking a group of individuals, discovering and valuing individual talents - without suppressing, changing or diluting them - while maximizing them together in a playing system where the collective impact is greater than the sum of the individual parts.

Youth-team coaches also have a quality that has gone missing in other organisations - they spend the majority of their time really getting to grips with the human and technical resources at their disposal. Understanding them deeply, observing, studying the kids, so to maximize their potential.

There is a human side that is about character, suitability, attitudes, abilities, motivations and all of that quickly comes to the fore among children. You can observe and detect them pretty early.

There is a technical side that is about the approach to the game, the timely movements with and without the ball, and the skills in touching, treating and kicking the ball.

To learn this the coach needs to watch, carefully and over and over again.

Yes, I know I may have digressed a bit, but the notion of the team working with a specific framework and precise, unambiguous roles is very close to my heart because I believe that all organizations and companies should work in the same way. Same for the attitudes and approach of the best coaches, learning from the many I had the honour to observe throughout the years.

The culture and the behaviours within a company are heavily influenced by those leading them. I think we could learn so much from those who coach the kids, transforming them from boys having a kick-around into proper footballers and bringing them together in units which then become teams. We had a lot of coaches. It would be impossible to describe all of them.

We have already spoken about the first one when talking about the first day and the smell of the grass.

He was Mr. Cesarino Cervellati and had been a great player. Bologna born and bred, he spent the first part of his working life as a player for Bologna, before then coaching kids in the academy. Three hundred appearances and 88 goals in Serie A.

Cesarino Cervellati (15 February 1930 – 13 April 2018)

But above all he was a great coach and a great man, who knew how to understand, watch and love children and their development. He knew how to motivate kids, inspiring them and developing them. He gave us our start in football, and he showed us the importance of immersing yourself in the game and in the grass, appreciating the little things that football offers – they're the most memorable aspects too.

I remember that he forced us all, from one day to the next, to do keepy-ups alternating between our right and left foots. From that moment on, you were no longer allowed to take two consecutive touches with the same foot. At first it seemed impossible, almost cruel. Then, all of a sudden, you get the hang of it, you get the pace, you synch the movement, and it becomes natural. Like everything in life, practice makes you perfect and I had finally some use for my left foot, on top of just walking on it.

Even Maxi learned.

Mr. Cervellati would be badly needed today for some pros who lose their step for the fear of kicking with the other foot.

With Mr. Cervellati we had also Mirko Pavinato, another legend in the Bologna football club history.

The captain of the Bologna team that won the last league in 1964. A tough defender and a coach with unique human qualities and with teaching skills on the fundamentals such as ball control and handling the ball with speed. At that time, it was normal to work a lot on the technical fundamentals, especially on the control of the ball and short passes. All things that I can't see today attracting the same attention.

Mirko Pavinato (10 June 1936 – 7 March 2021)

After Mr. Cervellati, while we were still with the "Pulcini", we were then coached by Mr. Anleri. How lucky were we! He was the right man for the job – a good coach, a kind man and he really managed kids well, striking the right balance between work, commitment, and fun. It's not easy to find the perfect blend when you're eight and you want to learn and develop, but also to have a lot of fun and enjoy the game.

But more than anything he knew how to handle the parents, who were obviously just getting to grips with tactical decisions, substitutions, starters and reserves. It's the first time you're faced with a team hierarchy. That's important inside a team and outside one too.

It sounds impossible but the parents need to get an education even more than the kids on this. I realised that the first time I saw my son Mattia starting from the bench. That was inconceivable to me because he was obviously the best player on the team in my eyes... as a father.

With Mr. Ballardini and Mr. Rigosi we learned how to set up, how to position ourselves on the pitch in terms of spacing, how to create space and how to shut it down to slow or halt the opposition.

For the first time we learned what it really meant to play without the ball.

That's not a very easy concept for a 10-year-old to grasp. I mean, when you have the ball, you play football, because you kick it. But what are you playing when you don't have the ball? There was an underlying issue of logic and also willingness because we were there "to play football" and so we needed to get on the ball. That's it. Otherwise, we would take up running or athletics. But in fact, we learned that even when you don't have the ball you can move to make life easier for your teammate to pass it to you or even to "show" for a pass.

How incredible to think that you could speak to a teammate without even breathing a word to him. Just like magic, football became a language, a means of communication.

It became like telepathy!

You make a run into space; he spots you and plays you in.

And you score.

Cool!

Without speaking.

Understanding one another without speaking is an amazing feeling. It's a bit like friendships – it tells you so much without ever saying anything.

But it was even more amazing when we finally discovered a practical use for something they called a "diagonal" at school. Finally, we'd learned something useful at school.

I will always remember the look in Ballardini's eyes, his intensity and his facial expressions. He could strike fear into you with just one look. And the great thing was he would even do it when he was joking around. And it wasn't always easy to tell which was which.

In the Esordienti age groups we developed as a team. There was always a core of 12 of us from a total of 18 players, while the others would come and go. From time to time, some of us would go and play up with the older guys, especially the more physically developed.

Those were the years of the unbeatable team. In those years from the "Esordienti" to "Giovanissimi" age groups with coaches Mr. Rigosi, Mr. Donini, Mr. Bonini and Mr. Mucchi, it was time to learn how to move as a unit: to keep the distances and the team shape; to begin playing the offside trap; to stay compact as a unit and get as many bodies packed into a tight area of the pitch as possible to give us a greater chance of winning the ball back and in turn make it easier and quicker to play a pass.

They began to expect us to play the ball on the ground and never launch it long. Or rarely at least. Because when required Marione and Maxi would happily punt one into the stands. They used to relish it.

The step up to the "Giovanissimi" (under 14) age groups was fairly traumatic for me. The Bologna academy had a supervisor called Bonini. A former Bologna footballer, he was an older man of 55-60. He was very good at his job but also extremely strict and tough. He didn't coach a single side but oversaw them all. He was not coaching a specific team or age group; he was supervising all teams. As it was for Mr. Cervellati and Mr. Pavinato, he had a very strong charisma.

One day he took me to one side, and he said something to me that made me feel so uncomfortable that I was afraid to talk about it. Especially with my parents because I was afraid of how they might react. So, I didn't talk about it with anyone.

It was the start of the season and I had known him for a few years, but we had never had a serious conversation besides the usual chat during training and matches.

I was 12 or 13 and it was the year after the Esordienti age group, a year after the unbeatable team and we were at one of the first training sessions of the year as "Giovanissimi."

It was Virtus' ground, via Valeriani. I was a very attacking right winger and sometimes I even played at centre-forward.

He took me to one side in midfield – I still remember the exact spot on the pitch as if it were yesterday – and he said to me, "This is an important year and we'll be able to tell if you have what it takes to make it as a footballer. That's why we're going to do two things. The first is you will train and play with the older boys. The second is you need to learn how to defend and how to play on the left, so you will be playing left-back."

That was pretty traumatic for me. First because I didn't really want to change position and move from attack to play at the back. But above all because playing up with the older kids, 1 or 2 years older, meant I wouldn't play with my mates, my friends. My best friends. And I didn't like that one bit. What's more, we occasionally played against the older kids, and I didn't really like them. Or at least I thought I didn't, as we were used to playing against each other all the time in training matches.

But what really shook me came later and I will never forget any single word. "Because we want to turn you into a professional footballer..."

When I heard that, I burst into tears.

Just like that. In front of him. Like a fool. It was a horrendous scene, and I would push the button "delete all" from my memory tape. Where is that button?

Sadly, that moment is locked in my hard drive forever.

It was all very strange. I was leaving my friends to join the older boys and I was leaving the forward line to play at the back, yet it was all for something that I had always dreamed about. It was a confusing cocktail of emotions.

Too much. All in one go.

There were too many conflicting emotions for me to handle all together.

I had someone in front of me that believed I could make it and someone who would make my dream come true, along with tangible proof that what I had dreamed about might actually be feasible. Or at least it was becoming suddenly more realistic than before.

But another thought came to mind that dominated everything else. I dreamed of becoming a professional footballer and playing for my country. I even went as a far as practising in my room various celebrations, so that I would be ready for the day I eventually scored in the World Cup final.

But deep down I knew that ultimately it was a dream that would never come true. "Because I can't be a professional footballer, I have to keep studying and who's going to the break news to my parents? My mum will be heartbroken... become one of those eleven men that kick a ball around in their underpants."

My tears were straight from this confusing mix of emotions.

The harsh reality that shackled the dream. The logic that snuffed out the passion.

I still remember Mr. Bonini's face when he stopped talking and he saw me start crying after he'd said, "Because we want to turn you into a professional footballer." He made a face like, "This kid is a complete idiot. I tell him that we think he can make it as a footballer, and he starts crying..." I remember thinking back a few days later, "How humiliating, he expected me to be tough, but I came across like a mug."

I just felt stupid.

Anyway, that year I played up with the older kids.

And I played all season wearing number 3, left-back. I'd never used any number below 7 so far.

It was so weird seeing the pitch from that side.

I must admit Mr. Bonini certainly had a good eye.

As a right winger I was already pretty dangerous once I got moving, thanks to my acceleration combined with ball control on the run. But his idea of playing me 30-40 yards further back was genius because there were three obvious benefits that were pretty breakthrough.

First, I had a lot more space to run into. For players who can run with the ball at pace, the more space you have to accelerate into, the greater the advantage of speed you take on your opponent who has a standing start.

Second, starting from deeper made me a lot more unpredictable. Because I didn't have a fixed marker, no one ever picked me up and that meant I could run at midfielders and defenders without them ever getting to grips with me. And so, no one could stop me.

Third, by starting on the left and cutting inside on my right foot as the wingers pulled wide, it was very easy to open up opposition defences and half the time I would get into a shooting position. Because when someone unmarked drives inside at you at pace having already picked up speed over 20 yards while the strikers pull wide, it opens up so much space.

It was an outstanding season.

I must admit Mr. Bonini was right.

Maybe I did have what it takes.

GIOVANISSIMI (UNDER 14)

The following year, the second one in the "Giovanissimi" age group (12 to 14 years old) did not start well. In fact, it couldn't have begun any worse. In fact, it didn't get started at all.

A few days before the first game I suffered a really nasty injury - a complete and displaced fracture of my humerus, ulna and the olecranon in my elbow. Basically, I destroyed the elbow joint and for the last 33 years I have been carrying around an unknown number of screws and metal plates that were used to reconstruct it.

That kept me on the side-lines for around 5 months.

I was lucky that I almost recovered full movement of the elbow, despite the initial prognosis not being that rosy. My parents were told that it would be impossible to know before the operation whether or not I would be able to move it again.

I was at my grandmother's house in the countryside in Budrio and Maxi had come with us on that particular Saturday. And we only did one thing – we played football all day. Nonstop.

I remember that cross as if it were yesterday, just above my head, slightly behind me.

I was good at overhead kicks. The previous year during a league match, I scored a wonderful overhead kick straight from a corner that went in just under the crossbar. It was a great goal. My dad was there watching at Lunetta Gamberini pitch and I scored in the goal overlooking Via degli Orti. I was very proud of it because you didn't see many goals like that at our age.

On this occasion though I remember there was a touch of dew on the grass and I slipped as I pushed off the ground, falling down before I could finish throwing my arm back. When I hit the ground, my arm was still outstretched.

It was a disaster. I immediately knew that something had gone very wrong.

I can't remember how painful it was. I actually don't remember any pain really. In fact, I didn't remember anything for several minutes - it was all a blur.

Then I remember that my dad held a white handkerchief outside the car window and floored it to Rizzoli hospital, Bologna's main orthopaedic facility, while I kept my arm nice and still. I sweated so much for that 30-minute car ride that by the time we got there the passenger seat was completely soaking. I was still in shock and heavily dehydrated when I got to the hospital, due to a loss of a liquid that my body wasn't used to. It was time for an X-ray and a series of manoeuvres that I'll spare you the details of.

Shortly afterwards my mother arrived too and they explained to me that it was essential I undergo surgery to reconstruct the joint, but not before a few days had passed, so that a few bones that were still loose could realign.

They didn't know if I would be able to move my elbow again. I was 13.

I don't like the number 13.

The operation took 7 hours and was a surgical masterclass.

Professor Zinghi, a good friend of my father's, did such fine work that he earned an important article in a series of science publications. I contributed with various photos, X-rays and first-hand accounts, as I tried in any way possible to help anyone else in a similar situation. The operation was a miracle of science and skill.

You can't thank surgeons enough when they perform work like that. They make so many other jobs seem small and insignificant in comparison. I have always held doctors, surgeons and those who dedicate their lives to treating others in the highest regard, and I feel unconditional admiration.

During the month I spent in hospital following the operation, I met some incredible people and heard some incredible stories. I remember them every time I overreact about something.

A hospital is a place that stays with you. Forever.

I felt hard done by because of what had happened to me and yet at the same time I heard stories that showed how life can take away so much from so many people, for no particular reason.

Sometimes, randomly. At least that's how it appeared to me.

It was totally unfair.

It is totally unfair.

It was the first time in my life that I stepped into a world more serious than anything I could comprehend.

I just couldn't reconcile two things which, to my mind and to my logic didn't make sense.

On the one hand, I was afflicted by my injury; I felt hard done by and down in the dumps; I had suffered and was still suffering.

On the other hand, witnessing first-hand accounts much more serious than my own situation - which was ultimately turning out for the best - put me in a position I couldn't cope with. I had done nothing to warrant my privileged position over those other more serious conditions. I was merely fortunate amid a series of unfortunate events.

What happened to those people every day in hospital wasn't my fault but I felt guilty nonetheless.

At 13 I couldn't get my head around it. Perhaps I still can't to this day.

Either way I shut myself off from the world. I was very rude to everyone.

I just wanted to be left alone.

After more than 4 weeks in hospital I was discharged, I began physiotherapy and my second year of high school, one month late.

It wasn't an easy decision to begin playing football again, because my parents had also been fairly shaken up by that accident.

Anyway, we came to the conclusion that I could start playing again provided I wore an elbow brace, just a sort of a light elastic bandage. To protect it. To be honest, I think they made me wear it to help remind me to be careful. But 30 stitches would have been reminder enough.

It was already January by the time I re-joined the team, 5 months on from the start of the season. It was our second season in the Giovanissimi, and I would be playing with my friends again (the unbeatable team from the Esordienti age group!) because the previous year I had played with the older guys.

After that injury I was delighted to be back among my friends.

I was happy.

I had football. And I had friends.

It was a great season and we won loads. There was me, Maxi, Ricki, along with Maldini, Marione, Cecconi, Ricci and Righi. Some other very solid players were brought in like Minghelli, a powerful midfielder, plus Vigherani also came back to play for us. He was an incredible striker - he always knew where the ball was going and scored every goal you could think of with every possible part of his body. He was one of those players who was always in the right place at the right time. One of those strikers who aren't particularly technically gifted, but they are natural-born goal scorers. He earned the nickname "Big Foot." A goal scorer's instinct is a concept you can only grasp when you see players like him in action. Guys that are just randomly wherever the ball drops. And when it happens time and time again, it's no longer luck but it's talent. You can't make it up. And you understand it when you see it for real.

It was my first season as a central midfielder, playmaker. It might just be my favourite position and the one where I remained for the rest of my "career" besides occasionally operating slightly wider in central midfield.

Playing as a playmaker for me was a bit like living in a mathematical equation. I was very good at maths. Partly because I was naturally good at it, and partly because my grandmother, Albertina, from whom I took my name and more besides, was a maths teacher. In the summer at her house in the countryside 20km from Bologna city centre, when I wasn't playing football, she used to challenge me with increasingly complex equations. She would always throw in something new that I hadn't studied. She did that so I had to come up with my own solution, without following rules but simply by using my own logic. That forced me to find new solutions and above all to understand what I was doing, as opposed to simply applying rules. We challenged each other at equations. I remember once that same year, in the second year of high school, I solved a very complex geometry problem in which I found the length of the diagonals in a complex figure. It was a theory we hadn't studied yet and I solved the task in class in a couple of steps. Something far above and ahead of any expectation for that task.

I remember it well for two reasons: firstly, the teacher gave me a mark of 10/10; secondly my classmates complained that it wasn't fair as marks usually ranged from 4 to 8 (despite the range was technically 0-10) and, therefore, I couldn't get a 10.

Crazy.

Years later, having lived abroad for many years and watching how people from other countries behave, I've thought about this problem as a very Italian trait. It's almost as if for many people it was more important for them to limit other people's success as opposed to working towards their own. This is not something I've seen elsewhere, and I still don't understand it.

Anyway, I kept the 10. On that occasion, my classmates could "do one."

But it really upset me. Because lots of them were my friends.

Anyway, playing as a playmaker was like a balanced equation for me, a geometry problem to be solved. The number of passes you receive must always be equal to the ones you play. If there's a difference it means you've lost the ball a few times.

And you can't ever lose possession in that position. Never.

It was the position that keeps the team's shape and pace of play. It was the position that sets the tempo, that defines the space in which the team operates and decides when to move through the gears.

Ricki played just to the right of me and he was getting quicker and more powerful all the time. Plus, his vision had improved. Maxi was always asked to deal with the opposition's most dangerous forward. I think he knew them all and they all knew him too. To the extent that sometimes before we kicked off, he would recognise the opposition forwards and tell the coach who should mark whom.

By that stage we were fully-fledged footballers - we knew how to play in different formations, we could move the ball and reorganise our shape during matches. We did well both in the league and the most prestigious tournaments, against the best sides in the local area.

We cruised to the league title and we won the Savena tournament, beating Casalecchio 4-1 in the final at the Pontevecchio ground. In that tournament I was picked for a select XI to play against AC Milan's "Giovanissimi" side.

Towards the end of the spring, it was time for the Villanova tournament which always made us really nervous. It featured the best teams and the pitch was really small which meant there was less space and your touch had to be flawless. The fence outside the pitch was basically only a yard away from the touchline and you basically had to take one-step corners. Around the same time there was also the Castelmaggiore tournament, where we made it to the final before losing on penalties. In that match I hit a shot that struck both posts. Sometimes it's a matter of millimetres.

They were our first evening tournaments. We played under floodlights, which was really exciting, as they felt like European Cup nights and the stands were fairly full given how important some of the matches were. They were certainly full of plenty of scouts. And at that age some of the players' sisters or female friends might show up. We were 14 years old, and their appearances started to become a matter of real interest in the locker room conversations.

Some players were more interested in the scouts. Others paid more attention to their teammates' and opponents' sisters.

It was the start of a new phase. Perspectives were moving and changing. And we were changing with them.

Our formations became more complex. Tactics became increasingly sophisticated and required even more physical and mental energy.

New dynamics also emerged off the pitch which were relentless and unstoppable.

In the summer of that year, I went to Gothenburg in Sweden to play in an amazing tournament. It was called the Gothia Cup, also known as the "World Youth Cup".

What a crazy competition. That year there were more than 700 teams hailing from more than 30 different countries. These days there are more than 1,700 teams from more than 70 countries around the world. All of the schools and youth hostels in Gothenburg were set up and each classroom was kitted out with 25 fold-out beds for the players and staff of every team. So there was something like 60-70 teams of 14-16 years olds staying in every school across the city.

On every classroom door, which became dorms, there was big sign with the name of the team on it.

There's one last thing I should mention. The teams were both male and female, all together and mixed in every school.

During the day we'd play football on the pitches then, back to the school, we continued to play in the school field, together with the guys or girls from all the other teams.

That was football in its very best as a universal language.

Alternatively, we'd all head into town dressed in our tracksuits. The entire city was completely invaded by boys and girls in coloured training outfits.

In the evenings we would meet up, have parties, listen to music and camp out together.

It was amazing. So many young people, all brought together by football. I don't remember any fights or anything really serious or crazy happening, because football was everything to us.

Then obviously when you put 1,500 teenagers together, naturally there's a buzz about the place.

Anna was a midfielder for Munksund-Skuthamns, a team from a town in the north of Sweden called Piteå. We liked walking in the school grounds hand-in-hand until we reached a point where you could see all of Gothenburg.

That was it.

But my heart was beating, as when you run the entire field and you reach the line left with only one breath to cross it.

For more than a year we wrote each other letters, proper hand-written letters where you lick the envelope to seal it and you need to buy a stamp before to post them, hoping that they will get to destination. And who knows when.

You had to sweat them, as many other things of life.

They were not the mail where you just need to push the icon "send."

Every time a letter came through the post, I felt like my stomach was imploding.

I couldn't explain it.

Then there came a time when we stopped writing to each other. But I left the sign with the name of her team stuck on my bedroom door. I stole it on the last day of the tournament. It was a footballing memory and it was the memory of a whole new feeling.

Like when you pick the ball up and you place it on the penalty spot.

You feel your insides churning.

Your heart skips a beat.

It takes your breath away.

It will finish a few seconds, but you will remember it forever.

PARTING WAYS

At the end of the "Giovanissimi" age group, just before we all turned 15, the Bologna academy came to an end and you had two options.

If you were signed by the youth teams of a professional club like Bologna, you began training with them in their "Allievi" side before hoping to move into the "Primavera" (U19) and then eventually the first team.

Conversely, other amateur or semi-professional teams might approach you to sign for their youth teams and then hope to move to a professional youth team some years later.

The coaches and scouts at the Bologna academy obviously had first refusal when it came to assessing us because we were already registered with the club as we played for their academy. So towards the spring of the last season as "Giovanissimi," the Bologna scouts - besides tracking our progress all season along with the scouts from several other clubs - set up two trial matches.

The first was on our pitch, at the velodrome, where all of the guys in our age group played. After that only a few guys were invited to Casteldebole for another mixed game against guys from several other teams.

I played the first one as centre-forward and even scored two goals and I played on the left wing in the match at Casteldebole.

I played well in both.

I remember that on my way home from one of the matches, we were in the car with Maxi and while his mother drove, he confidently said, "Albi, you've definitely made it!"

At that level I did feel I had an edge as having played for two years with the older "Giovanissimi" side I had gained some experience. Then there was my growth spurt which had seen me gain an inch or two on my peers.

So basically, everything had come together and if Maxi said that I'd definitely made it, then it would surely come to pass.

It didn't. I didn't get picked.

I didn't make it and nor did Maxi or Ricki.

I never did get my head around it.

They picked Ricci and Vicki who both deserved it because they were really, really good, probably the best of our group. But I wouldn't say they were completely on another level to us, as we all had a mix of physical attributes and footballing ability which were above average for our age group.

We discussed it many years later too, during one of our "three-man weekends" that I'll cover later in the book, debating what it was we were lacking to cross the motorway that separated Bologna city centre from the training ground at Casteldebole. But we never did find an obvious answer.

It's also true that the rumours were that only the very best players were signed by Bologna (and we saw some of them), or alternatively the ones who were given a big helping hand (and we saw plenty of those, some of whom would have been on the bench 10 times out 10 for us). And our parents certainly did everything but push in that direction. Quite the opposite.

I don't think that was the main reason, but I did have my doubts in the subsequent years, having heard my parents talk about "what had and hadn't been said" on the matter. There were a few times when they very quickly changed the subject, which made me think that something had gone on, but I was never told what that was.

At age 15 it wasn't easy to juggle a tough high school with 3 hours of training every day, on top of an hour commute. It was very clear to Maxi and me (at high school "Fermi") and Ricki (at high school "Righi") and above all to our parents what the priority was—to study and to take a university degree.

There comes a time in life when you find yourself at a crossroads and you have to make big decisions. You often aren't in control of the situation and there are lots of small details that only make a minor difference on that specific day but create a gulf over the long run. It's like two straight lines that start from the same point. They are slightly angled and at first they meet, then gradually they begin to move away from one another, yet remain close before becoming increasingly far apart. After a long while they will be very far from one another, even if the initial angle was very slight.

So, on day "zero" on that afternoon in May at the end of the Giovanissimi season, the difference between becoming a footballer and an engineer was miniscule. It was the starting point from where those two separate lines run and they move from the same point, in the same place at the same time. To the extent that they meet. But 20 years later the gap which was barely there at the starting point becomes a chasm.

Anyway, for whatever reason, that day those lines separated ways.

There will be a moment that they will cross again a few years later.

Lots of teams were interested in us and we got lots of phone calls at that time. Almost all the best clubs in the city were interested in the players in our team, because at youth level we were the side with the best results and we caught the eye of lots of clubs.

Some clubs were keen on some of the players and not others. And then there were even some that were interested in just one of us three, so we would have had separate ways.

Obviously, there were lots of things to weigh up, like the professionalism and ambitions of the club, the division the first team played in - that could range from the fourth to the eighth tier - and where the team trained and played their matches. The last point was very important to our parents, given that we were all 14 and so we would either travel there by scooter or get a lift from them.

In general clubs were fairly selective in their approach and they would focus on two or three players, but there was one team that stood out because they worked differently.

In fact, they ran a session where they invited as many as 8 players from our team along with our parents to a presentation, showing interest in all of us. It was basically the traditional core of our team. It was the year that the team was being re-founded by merging with two well-established clubs in Bologna (Croce Coperta and Turris Romea) to become one big club which would obviously be called Croce Coperta Turris.

They trained on a nice ground which was next to the gym where Virtus Bologna basketball team played. They also had a nice pitch, at least between August and October and then again from April onwards, and the match pitch was different from the training pitch, 70% of which was made up of clay.

I liked that pitch because just a few weeks earlier I played the final of the high school tournament there and my team, H section, won the tournament for the first time ever. I was in the second year of high school and I was given a trophy for finishing as top scorer. We went on to win the competition every year from the second to the fifth year of high school. Every year. We were the most prestigious house in terms of what mattered most at high school: winning the house football tournament which was made up of 16 teams.

To my mind, that pitch brought me good luck.

So, eight of us kids turned up to this meeting with our parents in a lovely clubhouse just outside Bologna.

The club president was there, along with the sporting director and one of the coaches. Only the sporting director spoke and he exuded charisma, although I couldn't quite figure him out. I felt like there was another side to him. He was one of those people who seem in control, clear and almost perfect in their ability to express their thought process. So perfect it's almost unnatural. And not completely transparent in any case. At that time, I didn't know how to qualify my gut feeling because I had very little experience with reading people. Either way he seemed a bit crafty in both the positive and negative sense of the word.

He told us about the merger plans, which had already been finalised, and the club's ambitions. But above all he confirmed that they wished to sign all of us to play for their Allievi Regionali side. Given that we had just played our last year in the Giovanissimi age group, as of the following season we were eligible for our first year in the Allievi, which was normally the Allievi Provinciali. But they were planning to promote all of us to play in their Allievi Regionali, which was the highest level of the Allievi age group for non-professional clubs.

It was a great league.

You would see players that would achieve good things in the game and that included guys who might re-join the youth teams of professional clubs.

It was an even more interesting proposition because of the playing style the coach wished to implement. He was seen as a strong coach, a proponent of zonal marking and practised a very modern brand of football, with organised attacking play.

Either way, those were all just minor details. The truth is that the chance to all stay together as a team was the main factor for all of us and it was practical move too because they were based in the city and not a million miles away from where we all lived.

We decided to go, the lot of us.

Apart from Maxi.

I don't really recall why Maxi went against the grain. Maxi was very attached to our group of players, and I was amazed by his decision. But I think it was because another club, BoCa-Sparta, were really chasing him to play for their Allievi Regionali side and their first team played in the sixth tier. In contrast, Croce Coperta and Turris Romea before the merger and the expectations to move up significantly, were bouncing between the seventh and eighth division. This means that Boca, as a club and a first team, were at least a cut above.

Maxi decided to sign for BoCa and that would prove to be a temporary move, because just three short years later we were all back together again.

We all agreed and seven of us signed for Croce Coperta Turris.

These decisions were made before the summer. Then we all met up, first at the club offices, then for the first training sessions and finally it was time for the pre-season training camp in the mountains.

Before we all met up something unexpected happened which was very frustrating for me personally.

When they called us in to the club's offices for the first training session, I realised that the date and time I'd been given was different to the one all of my six friends had been given.

Just me.

All of the others met up at the same time on the same day, whereas I came in on my own on another day. I couldn't understand why. Unless I'd been picked for another team.

And that was exactly what had happened.

All of my friends were to join up with the Allievi Regionali. Whereas I would be with the Allievi Provinciali. Just me.

It instinctively felt like a punishment and the more I thought about it, like an insult. That's because I wanted to play with my friends and I had chosen the club ahead of countless other offers, so this was a punishment I didn't deserve.

It was an insult because in my mind I was the guy who had been told, just a few weeks before, "Albi, you'll definitely make it to the Bologna FC." A few months later, how was I the only one not with the Allievi Regionali? Maybe they'd only signed me because had I not gone, perhaps they would have missed out on some of the others? So they essentially used me but there weren't really interested in me?

That was the only explanation I could come up with. And that was the reason that someone at the club, who was fond of me, told me a few months later. Basically, the Allievi Regionali coach didn't rate me at all and didn't think I was suited to his style of play. But they knew that we were a tight-knit group and that I was the captain of that team and that my decision would in some way influence the others'.

I was distraught.

And I knew that it broke my dad's heart too seeing me like that.

I felt used. I felt humiliated.

Essentially, I had been cast aside for perhaps the first time in my football career. It had never happened to me before.

And even more importantly, I might not have ever played with my oldest friends ever again.

But at that stage, there was no other option.

Frustrated and a little humiliated, I started pre-season with the Allievi Provinciali. I didn't speak to the sporting director or the Allievi Regionali coach again after that. Not even two years later when I was the first of that group to become a regular fixture in the first team for the entire season.

I never needed to approach them, but nor did they ever make the first move with me. Maybe they at least felt a bit guilty about how they'd treated me.

Not once that season did they ask me to play the odd game for the Regionali. Not once.

Looking back, I was actually quite lucky. First of all because the lads in my new team were really nice guys and pretty good players too.

Second, because the coach, Maurizio, was a really good tactician but above all a brilliant people person. He was one of a kind. And he perfectly grasped the situation. He was able to help me rediscover my motivation. I became captain of the team and shared the armband with another great guy, Roberto. We were playing together in the midfield and we had an excellent harmony. He was a great player and a great guy. He was in that team for years, but he helped me greatly in coming in and finding support. Those are the unique and extraordinary facts about football. That bonding that comes from the instinctual ability to understand each other and the willingness to always support each other. He was not the only great guy. I could mention all, but I don't want to forget a few.

Third, because the coach of the Allievi Regionali wanted to play like Sacchi - all zonal marking, pressing and a compact unit. And he really thought he was like Sacchi but he really wasn't, besides being bald.

But the biggest issue wasn't that he thought he was Sacchi even though he wasn't, but rather that he didn't even realise he wasn't Sacchi. Good old self-awareness, over the years I learned how important it is to get to know who you are.

I think Ricki really struggled that season.

He had really bulked up but that had in no way affected his technique which had always been impressive. He also learned a lot from zonal marking, which requires much greater focus than traditional or man marking because you're always back there keeping your shape both when you have the ball and above all when you're not in possession. But that coach applied so much psychological pressure too. He was constantly shouting.

I think I know Ricki pretty well. And being shouted at is not something he has ever put up with. Ricki is someone who favours debate and dialogue and indeed he went on to become a lawyer. He wants to understand and hear someone else's point of view. He's open to criticism, but you can't shout at him because he'll shut himself off.

He'll close into himself. And he'll cut you off completely.

He couldn't have fun in those conditions, in that environment.

In the end, that season marked a total separation after many years.

Maxi to BoCa, Ricki and I in the same club, but Ricki in the Allievi Regionali and me in the Allievi Provinciali.

I couldn't tell you what I took from that year. I think the feeling of being used left me disappointed and humiliated. But it was not playing with my friends that hurt the most.

The following year I skipped the Allievi Regionali completely and went straight with Ricki into the Under-18s and then straight into the first team.

Maxi joined us the year after that.

Then in the middle of 1992, things changed.

In fact, they changed in the space of three days. Forever.

EVERYTHING CHANGES, IN 3 DAYS: TRIALS, KISSES AND LIGAMENTS

They say the darkest hour comes right before the dawn. That's probably true. But the opposite is also true—i.e., when you reach the top, you're best off putting on your parachute quickly as you can really come crashing back down to earth.

I don't know how things work, or if there's a logic that dictates circumstances and defines how they play out. But looking back, everything begins to make sense and it all seems more obvious now. Almost as if it were all predetermined. Or in any case, with the benefit of hindsight, it's that much easier to accept.

It all happened to me in the space of three days that changed everything.

That year, despite the fact that I was an Under-18 player, I had played the entire season with the first team. And I'd done pretty well too, scoring goals and setting them up and above all I became the team's mascot because I was the youngest one there.

They even wrote a nice article about me in the paper. I can still remember the headline "The right mix of ability and intelligence." In fact, I was doing well at school and I got good grades, despite not putting much work in. I did just about enough to continue my education with no issues, but without hitting the books so hard that I lost focus on my football. "Could do more" was the takeaway message every time my folks went to parents' evening at my high school. For five years straight. I only started to give 100% once I got to university.

But I played very well and I worked really hard on my game.

I remember picking up the call to speak to the journalist in my parents' bedroom, laid out on their bed focusing hard on my answers. I still have a copy of the article in my desk drawer.

A few weeks later a life-changing opportunity came along. The club was contacted by Modena, a team in Serie B, because on the Tuesday of that week they were playing their weekly friendly at Crespellano, a team in the fifth division. It was strange that they were playing on a Tuesday, as ordinarily those matches would be played on a Thursday. It might seem irrelevant, but I remember it clearly because even a small detail and a slight anomaly like that would have enormous repercussions.

Both teams wanted to take a look at me.

There's a big difference between a team in Serie B and the fifth tier, but I never gave it too much thought. All that I cared about was going there and performing well, whatever happened.

I played the first half for one team and the second period with the other.

I played as a midfielder in the first half with Crespellano, alongside an unbelievable player. I still remember his name, Meletti, I'll never forget it. A few minutes after kick-off, I took a throw-in into his feet in midfield. Without even looking he touched the ball with his toe and moved his body back a fraction, just enough to nutmeg the player that was tackling him from behind.

With just one touch. Off his toe.

Mental.

He was definitely one of the best players I'd ever seen.

And he played in the fifth division.

I've always wondered what the difference is between a fifth-tier player and one who players in Serie A. I'm still not entirely sure if the difference is only technical or physical and psychological too. But I think at times there are lots of intangible factors beyond one's control that can make one career and break another, often with no rhyme or reason. Could it even come down to whether a match is played on a Tuesday rather than a Thursday?

Are there ever times when a scout attends a game and only arrives in time for the second half? Or a parent expresses doubts over the compatibility of high school and university and the youth academy of professional club? Who knows? Maybe it's a combination of all those things. Some will say luck, some others that you earn your luck.

Anyway, I played the first half for Crespellano and we played so well that we won it 1-0. We beat a Serie B team, who on paper were three divisions higher than us.

I had performed well, keeping it simple and playing neat and tidy. I took few touches and moved the ball quickly and precisely, holding my position and never finding myself short of breath despite the step up. I must say that playing alongside good footballers – and there are plenty of those in the fifth tier – is incredibly easy because they run where they're supposed to, they move into space and they feed the ball through at just the right second which gives you the edge on your opponent. But above all you always have a teammate in support when you need one, so it's a lot easier to play one- and two-touch football.

Playing with very strong players is far easier and makes you look much stronger as well. Great players make the team stronger and a great team makes each individual stronger.

I learnt it that day. That way.

In the second half, switching shirts, I made my "debut" for a Serie B side. I was finishing high school and about to start university, engineering. It was a great time in my life.

I was playing with well-known professionals. Or I'd at least seen them on TV in the brief highlights they showed from Serie B on a Sunday.

One of the best players was Caruso, a short, pacy second striker. He was your typical maverick; you never knew what he would do next and he would always change the tempo of your play. Then there was Provitali, a proper centre-forward, a real powerhouse; he wasn't quick, but he was always in the right position, he held the ball up well and he was able to make runs in the box and come short for the ball. Caruso and Provitali were an excellent strike pairing for a Serie B side.

They picked me at left wing and for someone who was used to playing central midfield, it wasn't easy at first.

But I was on fire.

The second half began, and we were 1-0 down to Crespellano. A few minutes later I set up the equaliser.

I remember the move as if it were yesterday.

The left-back played the ball down the line to me. I ran towards it along the flank with my back to goal, just inside the opposition half and I laid it off first time inside to Caruso. Rather than turning to break forward on the wing I ran diagonally infield towards the D and cut across the middle of the pitch. Maybe I did it instinctively because I wasn't confident about crossing from the by-line with my left. He laid it off to me through the middle four yards ahead of me. I reached it in a few short strides and without looking I played it through with the outside of my right foot, threading it into the path of Provitali two yards inside the box as he darted infield to my right. He controlled it on the run, shot and scored. Before I publish this book, that is if I ever do, I promise you I'll include a diagram.

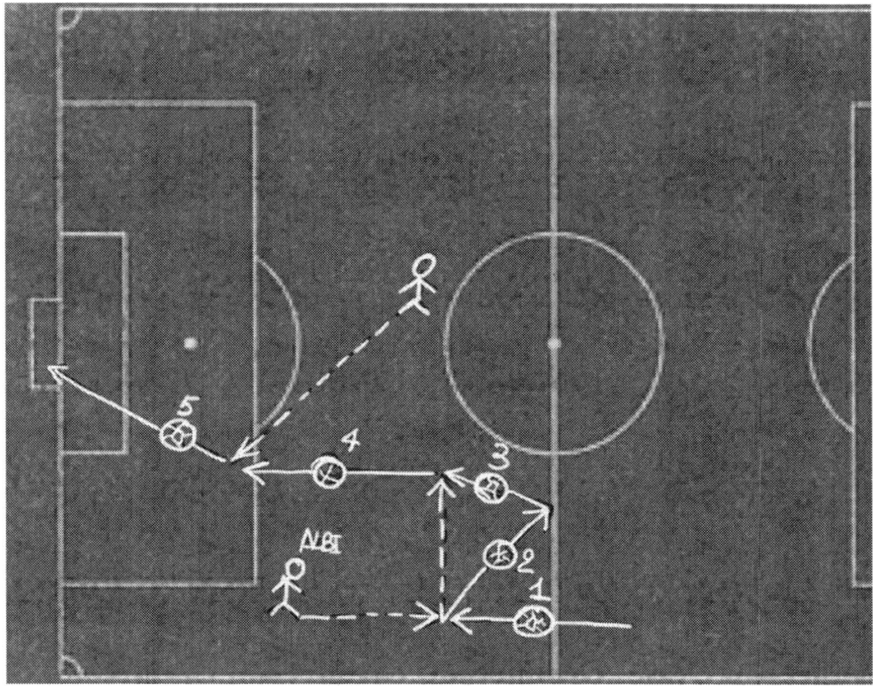

As promised – the accurate visualization of the dynamic.

Provitali gave me five and said, “Nice one, kid.”

Thank goodness for that. I produced an assist that couldn’t have been more inch-perfect even if I had a tape measure.

Fifteen minutes later came my masterpiece. A long ball was played down the left wing in behind the defence. I chased after it, brought it down with the outside of my right boot and with the inside of my left I fizzed one across the top of the grass, like a stone that gathers pace as it skims across the surface of the water. It was a lovely ball curling away from the keeper down the "corridor of uncertainty” right, into the path of my teammate running on to it. It was one of those inviting balls in that by the time they reach you, you either smash it home or launch it into the car park.

Caruso smashed it home.

Playing left wing wasn’t half bad!

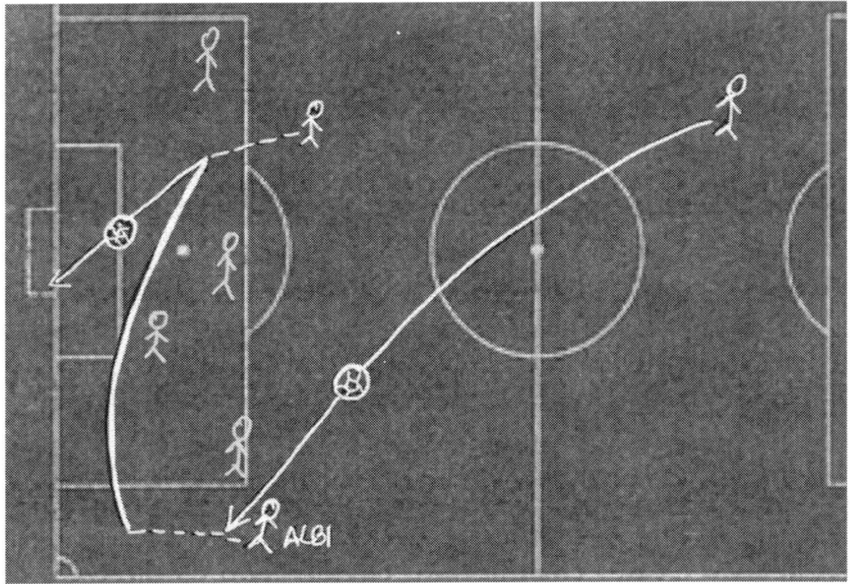

I am starting to enjoy these diagrams

I played two halves for either side, winning both games, and produced two assists I'll remember forever. Legendary.

It was Tuesday 21 April.

The following day, the Wednesday, I met my girlfriend at 2pm to break up with her.

Yes, because two hours later, at 4pm I had to meet another girl who I really liked. She was a really nice girl, blonde, but above all she smiled like no one else. And for someone like me who doesn't smile much, it was like seeing the sunshine cut through the fog of the Padana valley. We shared our first kiss.

I will always remember that I kept looking into her eyes while I kissed her because they were beaming.

Twelve years later she became my wife. Sixteen and eighteen years respectively later she became the mother to my children. Everything good I've done in my life has been with her.

It was Wednesday 22 April.

Two unforgettable days.

That same day the Under-18 coach called me to ask if I could play the next match for the Under-18s rather than the first team, because they were going well and were in the hunt to win the title, whereas the first team would finish in midtable and didn't have much left to play for.

So rather than training with the first team on the Friday, I would train the previous day, Thursday 23 April, with the U18s who all my friends played for. I couldn't wait. Especially because Ricki was there.

I didn't tell them what had happened with Modena and Crespellano; I just wanted to play football with my mates.

During the training game to finish the session, Ricki took a corner from the left. The ball dropped to me outside the box, I controlled it and held off the defender with my back to goal. As it bounced, I went to lift it over the defender with a sombrero to turn him before collecting it on the other side and shooting at goal.

I never did take that shot.

After I lifted it over the defender's head, my foot stayed rooted to the ground for a millisecond longer than it should have done before my knee could stop twisting.

The pain was impossible to describe. Ricki was stood by the corner flag on the opposite side, yet he heard that I'd broken something. That's what Ricki told me.

I lay on the ground screaming "Don't touch me, don't touch me."

I don't remember anything else.

I don't remember going back into the dressing or going home. I can't remember anything. I've generally got a good memory. There's a film by David Lynch called "Eraser head." That sums it up. It's all erased.

But the biggest break is yet to come.

You realise that nothing will ever be the same again. That you will never be the same again.

The following morning my dad took me to Bologna's most-renowned knee surgeon. The guy that had helped Roberto Baggio get fit again. It only took two movements of my knee and all of five seconds for him to purse his lips beneath his moustache and say very matter of factly, "Ruptured anterior cruciate ligament. I can operate as early as tomorrow if you like."

I'll never forget that. I burst into tears.

The following Monday that man with the moustache reset my anterior cruciate ligament with a strip taken from the tendon in my knee cap. I later learned that it was a fairly experimental procedure at that time, and I was one of the first to undergo it. Either way it didn't turn out as well as I'd hoped and a few years later I had to go through it all again, this time with another technique, using the gracilis and semitendinosus tendons which thankfully proved more durable.

I like to think that had it not been for that injury, I would have become a professional footballer and a very good one at that.

I like to tell myself this little white lie.

It might even be the only fib I still afford myself as an adult.

That was my sliding doors moment and maybe we all have one. Over the years what you lose in terms of energy, you more than make up for in perspective. And perhaps for all of us, with a bit of perspective, looking back, we can all put our finger on those few seconds, few short minutes or those three days in which everything changed.

I don't know. The only thing I do know is, over the course of those three days, everything changed.

Forever.

THE BLUE CLIO

In the 1980s there was a science fiction film about a huge portal that transported people from one dimension to another, to far-off time periods and far-away planets. Maxi, Ricki, and I all loved sci-fi, as long as it wasn't better than Star Wars because that would have just been too much.

That would have almost been insulting.

And unlikely anyway.

It was a nice concept. On the one hand there was a civilised people who were technologically primitive (us humans) and on the other a horde of coarse, wandering barbarians who were at the cutting edge of technology.

It was basically a little like the story of Giovanni Trapattoni's Juventus and Roma under Nils Liedholm. I'll let you decide which is which.

Anyway, it was an original idea with a good cast and lots of publicity – one of those films where they spend more on marketing it than they actually do producing it. A bit like the signing of Socrates at Fiorentina. Shall we compare him to how Giancarlo Marocchi performed at Bologna that same year or how well Eraldo Pecci played for the three after that?

Let's be serious here.

That pretty much sums up the 1980s. A triumph of marketing and communications, of fluff over substance and the massive boobs on the TV show “Drive in.”

Berlusconi* what a genius! (*He was the owner of the TV channels that revolutionized TV entertainment in the 80s). Say what you like about him, but you can’t say he didn’t understand what people wanted both in business and politics. And in football too, both in terms of an innovative brand of football and based on the results he got.

Although it’s not as if social media in the new millennium has helped deal with people’s instinct to be in the public eye from the 1980s. Quite the opposite.

Social media might even seem classier than "Drive in” on the channel "Italia 1” at 8:30 on a Sunday night. Or at least more technological and definitely smarter. Ultimately though it has allowed everyone to create and build their own perception of what society looks like, to showcase their talent, share news and stories of all types with no limitations. Perhaps it has taken a human skill (proving you got there first) and made it more democratic and tacitly accepted by the social community. Because, let’s be honest, people spend more time posting the worst things imaginable rather than thinking about their own physical and mental well-being. Which seems unfathomable when you think about it.

At least the boobs in "Drive in” were real. They might have had a helping hand from a surgeon, but it wasn’t like they stuffed their bras or anything.

Anyway, this film had none of the magic of Star Wars.

But I digress.

But we actually did have our own portal that transported us to another dimension.

Our blue Renault Clio.

Ricki used to drive it. It was after all his car, but he was actually the one who least liked driving it. Yet at 7:10pm (actually 7:15 – I'll get to that in a minute) he was always there in Piazza Trento Trieste, followed by Maxi.

I was always the last there.

And they used to give me stick for it. But when you're in the middle of trying to solve an equation on structural mechanics, it's not as if every second counts. "Give me a break – I'm out here saving the world." Because the solution always came right at the last minute.

In fact it was so unfair that they would give me stick, because officially they'd arrange to meet up with me at 7:10, but at 7:15 between themselves. So when I showed up 7:15, I was actually bang on time. They never did tell me that.

Arseholes.

Then, wouldn't you know it, I ended up moving to Switzerland for nearly 15 years where you can't survive unless you learn to be on time. Just try and walk into a shop in Geneva two minutes before closing time. They'll give you your marching orders even if you want to swipe your credit card in exchange for a €2,000 pair of shoes, something that by the way I have not even tried, and I don't believe I will ever do, but it was normal to see this type of purchases in Geneva.

Anyway, our Clio blue, as the doors were shut, was taking us to another dimension. The three of us, football and life and we left everything else behind.

The blue Clio was taking us somewhere else.

Into our own world.

A bit like the tunnel from the dressing room—you know where it begins but you don't know where it ends. Because there's no end to the football pitch. The white lines demarcate it, but they can't contain it. Ever.

From 19:15 to 19:45 the blue Clio was filled with stories, debates, anecdotes and occasionally deep intellectual discussions such as the one about the best forms of contraception, including the one about "the jump of the quail" that was triggering intense emotional and rational disputes on the risk and the cruelty of such athletic gesture. I still find very debatable the opinion about reinforcing the six packs.

Tuesdays were usually a chance for us to critique our game from the previous Sunday, with random takes on our teammates' performances. Rather than their displays on the pitch, we discussed the dressing-room rumours about the Saturday nights of characters such as Bress and Angelini. Often the result was already a formality once they came into the dressing room and took off their sunglasses. That's when it dawned on us that we'd be a couple of men light.

Our views on Serie A focused on Bologna, obviously, and on Roma, the team I supported (besides Bologna), and at times on Sampdoria because they had Roberto Mancini who had been our hero when we were kids in the Bologna academy.

In 1982 when we were 8 years old, he was 18 and had already scored nine goals in 30 games for Bologna. We were always at the stadium, and he was one of us. He left us at the end of the season to win trophies for Sampdoria at home and abroad, alongside his strike partner Gianluca Vialli.

When we were kids, “il Mancio” was the embodiment of the gifted kid. And he has always been one of us.

On Fridays we looked ahead to the following Sunday. We didn’t weigh up the team we were due to meet but everyone had their own reasons for how they approached Sunday’s game.

Ricki remembered the quality of the pitch because he was more of an artist than a battler and always struggled on bad playing surfaces.

Maxi recalled that the centre forward was a massive wanker and so knew already that on the corners anything could have happened.

Whereas I remembered how far we had to travel because I was already stressed about my next exam and I would count the number of hours I had in which to study before and after the match. In truth, however hard I tried I wouldn’t ever open a book after a game, because the only mental strength I had left was used to remember where the jar of Nutella was so I could dip my knife and let all my fatigue out.

My brain could only process one thing: nothingness.

Sometimes on a Sunday night, I dragged myself out to eat a pizza - in fact it was not even pizza, we were in love with this weird massive panino made with pizza dough and filled with all sorts of ingredients - and watch a film at Cinzia's place in her loft. I remember suffering splitting headaches that would have my head spinning from one moment to the next. I used to drive home on my moped on autopilot like I was in a trance and I would be out like a light before my head even hit the pillow.

I was spent.

Thinking about it now, we must have travelled thousands of miles together, the three of us in the blue Clio between training sessions and matches. And while I'm writing this, I'm not sure we ever considered how we would make it up to Ricki in terms of petrol money. I'm not sure Maxi and Ricki ever thought about it. Probably not.

It's crazy to think about it 25 years on and I feel a bit guilty about it. I won't tell them as much – I'll let them see for themselves when they read the draft of this chapter. Either way I think it's exceeded the statute of limitations.

Plus, Ricki is a lawyer.

Another hot topic was the coach and his training methods. But we'll talk about that later.

One day we got in the blue Clio on our way back from training and after a few miles Maxi and I spotted one footprint on the windscreen, like when steam forms silhouettes. The footprint was directly across from the passenger seat, where I sat. I thought that it was looking a bit weird to find a footprint there, on the windscreen. But then after a second, everything became clear.

I turned to Maxi and, indicating the footprint, we began to exchange unmistakeable glances.

Then Maxi very casually said, "Listen Ricki, I was wondering what that smudge is on the windscreen. Could you have a look – I don't know what it is."

I saw Ricki giving a quick look while driving. Then another quick one.

Silence.

We stopped the car by the side of the road and for a few minutes we were incapable of moving on.

We were losing our senses due to the intensity of our laughter. I think that must be the definition of "dying with laughter." That feeling when you can barely catch your breath because for a moment you can't breathe. It really does feel like you lose your senses.

Then Ricki tried to deny the evidence. Something that made it even more hilarious.

Full time whistle. Game over.

Come on, let's pull ourselves together because we have to drive all the way home and it's already gone 11pm and I have to study...

THE TEAM '92- '98

When you think about a football team, you typically imagine a group of like-minded people who share the same goal, have a certain number of things in common (training sessions, matches, etc) and have a similar way and pace of life.

I thought like that too before I played for the '92-'98 team.

At 1:30 on a Sunday afternoon, 90 minutes before kick-off, the following players would turn up: you already know Albi, Maxi and Ricki. Usually on time and in fairly good nick. At the end of the day, we were reliable sportsmen.

Maxi might have been on the pull the night before, cracking on to a couple of girls he'd just met, but it always fairly harmless.

Ricki had probably been out with his long-term girlfriend to watch a film and for a kilo of ice cream, but what went on after the ice cream never was never revealed beyond the confines of the blue Clio.

Nine times out of ten, Albi would hammer the books about "Analysis II" or mechanical technology until about 2 in the morning, which was famously when he was most focused.

So, all things considered, we were ready to play football.

Zappaterra was already at the ground. For a few hours maybe. Our defensive midfielder. He was the nicest, kindest and most disciplined person I'd ever met.

Apart from Father Angelo, my parish priest.

Zappaterra was good midfielder. Short, stocky, quick but also really effective. He also had a good spring and could make up the 20cm height advantage his opponent had over him. He never won the ball, but he always challenged for it. Selfless, tidy, the man who broke up play.

Stagnone, the policeman, was always on time. I never learned whether or not he was a pen pusher, but having a copper in our ranks made us feel very safe, especially for the away trips to the "appennino modenese" (the mountain west of Modena) or the "bassa emiliana" (the flat area north of Bologna). Versatile, feet like a defender and always there to serve the team.

Once Bress turned up we knew how the game would go. A skillful centre forward with decent vision, he really was a good footballer. The only issue was he already packed his football kit in his car before his Saturday night out. You can guess the rest. He must have run 20km combined across the whole 34-game season.

There was an upside to that though.

A combination of his fitness levels, the way he dragged his feet, his lack of energy and the experience of a well-travelled footballer meant he was brilliant at winning penalties.

A sensation.

I've never seen anyone go down as well as Bress did.

He did it so naturally that even VAR would give a penalty. Smooth and never over the top. Seamless. Given he was good at protecting the ball, he knew exactly where to position his leg, ankle or foot to make sure the opposition player would catch him. And he always took the contact perfectly, going down as naturally as one of the greats.

In one season he won me 11 penalties. I scored every single one. That year I scored 11 penalties and hit the bar 11 times from free-kicks, nearly all won by Bress. I finished the season with 18 goals (11 penalties, 2 free-kick and 5 from open play) which was a pretty good haul for a central midfielder.

The problem was Bress only scored 3. And when your centre-forward only bags 3 all season, you won't go very far as a team.

The sweeper, Tucci, was the most bow-legged person I'd ever seen. We used to say that you could fit a dog with a broomstick hanging out of its mouth through there. He was the ideal partner at the back for Maxi. One time this guy caught Maxi with a bad tackle and Tucci sprinted from 10 yards further back to give him a kick up the arse. Just like that. He was sent off, but we all remember that incident fondly. Tucci was a great guy.

Angelini always turned up late. Completely out of breath.

He had lots of different jobs. I think that recently he was working as a bus driver and he said that he would chase loads of birds, even though technically the sign said, "Do not speak to the driver," which I also imagine meant that the driver wasn't allowed to try it on with female passengers.

I think.

He played left-back and you never knew which way the ball would go when he kicked it.

Once when playing a back pass, he pinged one into the top corner. One of the backroom staff, who was getting on a bit, stood up to celebrate as the place fell eerily quiet. He shouted in a typical slang from the area of Bologna, "Va mo' la Angelini, soccia che goal!" which has some words in a tight Bolognese colourful language, but overall meant, "Look at that! What a fantastic goal Angelini!"

It was a hilarious scene. I'm still laughing about it now.

No one had the guts to tell him it was an own goal. Out of respect.

Another time there was the incident which will go down as the "sniper's shot." Angelo was bombing on down the left wing when he pulled his hamstring in such a quick, painful fashion, like whiplash, that it looked like he had been taken out by a gunman from the building overlooking the pitch.

He fell with his arms outstretched. Flat on his face.

Luckily the game was stopped for several minutes whilst he received treatment, because half of our team were rolling around. Laughing.

Angelini was blessed. Lots of people avoided taking a shower with him because it was pretty humiliating.

But the most amazing thing, or the second most amazing thing if you will, was that he was the biggest hypochondriac you've ever seen. "A clinical condition characterised by the excessive and unjustified concern over one's health or the health of others, with the belief that any symptom experienced by the individual is the sign of a serious ailment."

Over a 34-game season, Angelo would turn up almost every Monday to the department where Maxi's dad worked as a radiologist to get an X-ray of his ankle or a scan of his thigh or for an ultrasound on his sore hamstring. Every time.

Come training on Tuesday he would bring everyone up to speed on his condition. Plus, a detailed description of the nurse on shift.

We'll talk about Grazia in the next chapter.

Then there was Giallo. The keeper. He had a big sunny smile, but he was transformed on the pitch and he would have a go at our defenders, especially when they were out of position. The problem was, while he was good goalkeeper, he wasn't that good at calling defensive shape, so his instructions on who to mark were all over the place.

The ones I describe were the spine of the team. Adding then Maxi, central defender who played like a mix of Aldair and Pietro Vierchwood; Ricki, who at that time was dominating the right side, a little bit Cafu, a little bit Ryan Giggs; and me midfielder, I would say a bit of Kaka and a bit Giannini.

Then there was him.

The gaffer.

The gaffer was unlike anyone I'd ever seen in football.

He was a cross between Carlo Mazzone (especially in terms of how he looked) and Nereo Rocco (for the style of play, with a solid backline). He was always very tense and intense from the hour before training and matches to the hour afterwards, but for the rest of the time he was very kind and almost like a father figure.

Tactics were not his forte, but his fitness coaching took some beating: shuttle runs. We did thousands of them. There wasn't a single season, not even one, when someone didn't pull something. Hamstrings were going as often as Bressan went out clubbing.

I once heard him speak to the chairman and they were wondering why we had so many injuries. I'll tell you why. Because when you do 30 repetitions of 40 meters runs in progression every training session, hamstrings pop. That's why. That was it.

Besides that, Ronca was a good man. The sort that bonds with his players and loves them so much that the lines can become blurred, and he can seem more like a father to the players than their coach. That's understandable and even acceptable for a team, but it's not always productive.

We all loved Ronca and we loved to meet up with him. One of his favourites was when Ricki did his "giorgina" (when he started overdoing the showboating and for instance dribbled past the same opponent 3 times before being hacked down).

He couldn't wait for me to finish my exams, because for the week building up to them I was completely detached from the world, like I was in a trance.

He saw Maxi as the player that really epitomised his style of football: decisive, determined, sometimes rough and just hard enough to intimidate the opposition, but incredibly effective. Had the team pushed up a little more it would have been even better.

But I don't think Maxi saw things the same way because he was a brilliant marker, yet Ronca kept him on a tight leash. And Maxi had the ability to go forward from time to time. Maybe he could have gone up for corners because he could jump higher than anyone. But as far as Ronca was concerned Maxi wasn't allowed to go beyond the halfway line. That would have left us too exposed.

Formation? A 3-5-2 that became a 5-3-2 but could also morph into an 8-1-1 if we were under the cosh and it was time to launch the ball into the car park. Tucci was your man for that.

We had a few decent seasons, finishing between 2nd and 5th. So, always in the European places.

One year we made eight consecutive 0-0, Ricki and Tucci still talk about that each time we mee with the team every couple of years. They wouldn't have accepted bets for 0-0 any more. At the end of the season we could count only 9 goals conceded. We were by far the team with the best defense.

But we were horrible

A defensive bolt that would have been needed a chainsaw.

We only had one disastrous campaign and we were in danger of getting relegated until the final game. One of those matches where it's 35 degrees, it's all or nothing and you give it everything you've got. A memorable match in dramatic circumstances.

GRACE... AND TALENT

Andrea Grazia (literally in English translation "Grace") was a special guy. A great player and a one-off.

He was the oldest guy in the team, about 33, when Maxi, Ricki and I started playing regularly for the first team aged 18.

For us anyone above the age of 25 was "old." From time to time, we would look around the dressing room at the veterans, the guys who were 25 and above and above. They were all old, bald and for us they were already past it at that age. We wondered how they could keep playing.

Conversely, when we then reached their age, we still felt in peak condition, both physically and especially tactically. It was fun to watch kids of 19 occasionally put so much effort in for nothing. Greater experience of the situation would have allowed them to have conserved a lot of energy.

Andrea began playing football very late, almost by chance. And whereas millions of kids have to try their hardest and spend years practising just to control the ball once, he took up the game at age 14 and yet could control any ball coming from any angle with utter nonchalance and without the slightest bit of effort.

If a ball were pinged at him from the stratosphere, he would have brought it down without even looking. And without knowing how to do it.

But above all he would have done so without even the faintest idea of the piece of skill he'd just pulled off. And that's partly because no one had ever explained it to him.

Nor was he particularly passionate about football. He wasn't like other normal people who wouldn't have missed the Champions League final for anything, nor every goal on "90o Minuto" every Sunday.

He was nonplussed.

He was a self-taught player, a complete natural and completely unaware of his ability.

Or maybe he was aware, but he was nonplussed.

Or perhaps he did know, he just wasn't fussed.

One of the three.

Or maybe all three.

I remember a match in which I saw him emerge from a crowd of five players. He came away from there in the space of three touches, picked his head up and, with the outside of his boot, played me in to score. It was one of my first appearances for the first team. I still don't know how he came away from that group of players that looked more like a rugby scrum, so quick were his feet but as for the outside-of-the-boot ball to play me in, I saw that alright.

He didn't run across the ground, he glided. He had the same boots for seven or eight seasons. They were pristine. They looked brand new. Always the same pair.

Mine didn't last for more than a season. But he glided across the pitch without ever treading on it. He caressed the ball in the truest sense of the word. Maxi, Ricki and I said as much to each other so many times. We watched him closely. There was something inexplicable and unfathomable in the way he played football.

Andrea was intimidating because at times you didn't know where the ball was. You didn't see him move it because he shifted it so quickly between his feet. I used to steer clear of him in training because I was worried about injuring myself. Just in trying to win the ball off him you risked sustaining ligament damage.

He had only had one flaw. In fact, two. No, three.

The first was that he used to tuck his shirt into his shorts and wear them too high up his waist. It wasn't a great look. Let's just say it was fairly dated.

The second was that he used to stuff a handkerchief down his shorts. He had a white cotton handkerchief that he used to keep in his shorts and every now and then you would see him take it out and blow his nose. Then he would fold it up neatly again and put it back between his shirt and shorts.

I asked him once, "Hey Anda, what's the handkerchief all about?"

"To blow my nose," came his reply.

"Gotcha," I said. I didn't ask him anything else.

Third, he never went into a tackle. He never went down under a challenge, nor did he ever bring anyone else down. The story goes that he never once got booked in his entire career. Not even for dissent. When we had possession, it was like there were 15 of us on the team, but when the opposition had the ball we were down to 10, actually 9 if Bressan had been on a night out - so basically every Saturday.

A few years later Andrea suffered a serious accident when he was riding his bike. He was knocked off and sustained a serious head injury which left him in a coma for several days. He was left partially paralysed for a long time. He had to learn how to talk, write, walk and move all over again. But he came through it with a determination that only great men possess.

Hour after hour of work in the gym and pool, physical and mental exercises.

It was emotional to see him again two years ago as fit as a fiddle.

Maxi, Ricki and I often wondered how far Andrea would have gone had he began playing football at 5 rather than 14 and had he been fully aware of his talent. Or if he had approached training sessions and matches with the same desire and determination that he showed in clinging on to life after the accident. That revitalised him after his coma.

It's impossible to say with any certainty, but it's not beyond the realms of possibility to claim he would have been a great footballer.

Based on what we saw from Andrea, we thought the following about football: some players become professional footballers because they start with enough talent and they are taken on board by top-class academies and coaches from an early age, before being "built" into professionals thanks to years of work. Just like trying to do an "around the world" 100 times and finally managing it. Practice makes perfect.

Then there are those who are born with natural talent. A talent which is at times inexplicable and unfathomable and which is often not appreciated by those who possess it. A talent which at times is not expressed to its full potential because the individual is either nonchalant or completely unaware of the skills they are blessed with.

I wondered whether that was true in life too. At times life gives and takes with no rhyme or reason and I wondered how much of that is down to people being aware of their talent and ability as well as their desire to maximise it and determination to apply it.

Grazia was one of the most extraordinary talents I'd ever see play the game, but he didn't know that or he never realised it. Or he realised it but he never bothered to harness his talent to the fullest.

Whereas thousands of people try to push their limits, some people are born with talent which remains unfulfilled and goes unnoticed.

It's very difficult to say really what makes a real difference, when at the same time we see natural-born talents - players made from the determination to breakthrough - and footballers who are the result of just a great chance won. At the end, it's pretty useless to try to understand it. The result of the equation between talent, will power, and occasion will be different for everyone and each factor will have a different role. I always wanted to believe that there is no destiny and it's all in our control, and in our power. But is that the case with football careers? Or perhaps the round shape of the ball introduces new variables that will be impossible to calculate as well as to explain?

WAGS '92- '98

Thinking back now, the fact that Sundays, every Sunday, were sacrificed to amateur football and that our girlfriends, wives and parents also blew their afternoons with a blanket over their legs, or with the sun in their eyes, or even worse in the fog of the Po Valley, is verging on the ridiculous.

If the same thing happened to my daughter, I'm not sure I'd be completely on board. Or maybe I'd go along with her. Just a couple of times to see whether the guy deserved to be in the starting line-up or not and so if I can give him a chance.

Either way, that's what's so inexplicable about football: the fact it is able to dominate everyone and everything, and for nothing in return.

In the vast majority of cases, 99.9% of the time, those who play football whatever their age and the level they play at, go out there at the weekend for nothing. No fame. No glory. Very little money.

But you go out there and give it everything.

So it's a very simple equation: give everything, for nothing in return.

Yeah, that's right. That's what football is for 99.9% of those who play it.

So, the question then becomes, "Why?"

In fact, it's not quite "for nothing." In actual fact it comes with a cost.

Just to be clear, our girlfriends and parents used to pay to watch us play. There weren't discounted ticket prices for anyone. That was the same money that would eventually come back to us as a match bonus based on how many points we recorded each month. It would go up if we won and go down if we drew.

Basically, it would have been easier for our girlfriends and parents to pay us directly and we would have broken even. Deal.

But the true cost was greater still. Besides the ticket price, how about those weekends in May when the beaches of the Adriatic riviera are full? Whereas we would barely fill two rows of a tiny stand in Sasso Marconi if we were lucky. If we weren't it would mean a trip to places like Marano sul Panaro or Vergato, which would mean setting off at midday and getting home at 7:30 in the evening.

So, we would miss "90° minuto" on TV.

My dad and Maxi's dad used to arrive together in time for kick-off. They would share a lift because we basically lived next door to one another. Unless it was a long away trip, and, in which case, we'd all meet up and set off well in advance.

The stand would begin filling up with WAGS just a few minutes before a kick-off and a few minutes after they'd stopped by the bar.

The WAGS varied in terms of age, but all behaved in much the same way. That was a fairly interesting phenomenon in itself and I think it could be a nice topic for social scientists to study.

It was a very mixed group. From 20-year-olds Cinzia, Francesca and Ombretta, to the 30-somethings – Angelini's partner and the wives of Grazia, Zappaterra, etc – and the wives of the management and staff who were in their 50s and 60s.

They were the quite the sight. It was a real mixed bag.

It was interesting that the only time you could see differences between the various generations was before kick-off and after full time. Never during the game. When the match was on there was no difference either in terms of language or enthusiasm. I don't know whether that's a good or a bad thing.

I won't say anything more about the language they used, or how different generations tended to agree on certain points.

We could hear everything from pitch level. At times we weren't able to pinpoint who had said it, but we heard everything. And sometimes it was fairly embarrassing.

I've heard my fair share of bad language over the years, but nothing like the WAGS on away trips to the Bologna and Modena Apennines. I remember we used to laugh sometimes about what we heard coming from the stands.

There were times when it was freezing cold in the stands and they would share blankets and mulled wine. Then in late spring or summer they would choose to sit on the grass next to the pitch, which would be decked out in beach towels and full of brightly coloured bikinis and tiny shorts. It was all obviously just a way of distracting the opposition. I don't think they had a good view of the pitch laying out on all fours.

Cinzia once drove to the game because we were going out after the match. On the way out of the dressing room, the referee, who came from Modena, asked around if anyone could drop him off at the station. We were heading in that direction and so I gladly offered him a lift. There were no hard feelings about the pointless yellow card he'd shown me. Besides, I was captain, and I was well within my rights to point out that the criminal challenge on Ricki warranted a red for the opposition player. I might have been able to avoid throwing my hand up in the air and telling him to "F off" but that was just instinctive. I'd long since forgotten.

In football, what happens on the pitch, stays on the pitch. Or at least that's the intention.

We approached the car, I got in the front and I told Cinzia, who was driving, that we would be "giving this guy a lift to the station as it's on the way." In all fairness, the guy had a black bag with a long text on it saying "Italian Referees' Association"

"Sure, no problem," she said.

Cinzia and I didn't use to discuss the game on the drive home, because although she was happy to come and watch me play, she wasn't actually interested in dissecting the match.

But for some unknown reason, that day she decided to make some very pointed remarks: "You guys played well but that referee was a right mug. What game was he watching?" she said, perhaps expecting me to join in.

And join in I did, because before I burst out laughing, I just about managed to say loudly, "Maybe you should ask him yourself! He's sitting in the back!"

It wasn't a very nice incident; it was very awkward to say the least. For a fraction of a second, I scanned through the laws of the game in my mind to see if there was a section about "sanctions related to incompetent and/or distracted girlfriends" in the hope it wouldn't read "life ban."

Had it not been for Cinzia who, being well versed in awkward situations such as these (it wasn't her first time, nor would it be the last) drew a line under the incident by looking in the rear-view mirror and wisely saying, "Don't worry, I haven't got a clue about football."

The rest of the conversation was quite pleasant.

After we dropped him off at the station, Cinzia started having a go at me, saying that it was my fault because "You can't just let the ref get in the car without mentioning he's the ref and just referring to him as 'this guy.'"

She did have a point.

RAFFA'S JUMPS

It was the era of Zeman at Foggia, a few years later and we were 20.

I don't think there's anyone in the world who loves and understands football that wasn't impressed by the way that team played football. There were times when, once they really put it together, you almost couldn't understand what was going on, such was the desire, speed and determination with which they attacked.

He would do that all over again at Lazio, Roma and Pescara a few years later. Seeing 10 goalscoring opportunities in as many minutes was not something you were used to watching back then. And it was even more unusual to see the speed at which they played – it was like watching the match played at twice the pace, on fast forward.

The best description I ever heard of that brand of football came from my friend Silvio from Rome. He knew football inside-out: he had been a coach and he was a true football fan first and foremost. In his time off from being a Roma fan - very little I would say - he earned two degrees.

He pointed out that watching one of Zeman's sides play was really exhausting for fans too. That you needed a pre-season specifically for supporters. You were constantly up on your feet, before sitting down and getting up again because of the continual goalscoring opportunities. You'd see fans who were exhausted, sweating, and come full time they'd be absolutely spent, especially the old timers. It was like running a half marathon. People would pull a muscle from one move to the next because the team kept pouring forward. Forget doing squats. It gave you cramp just watching them.

The old timers could no longer handle it, even as the second half was starting.

We could go on a long tangent about Zdenek Zeman. You either love him or hate him. Some people quite rightly point out that he never won any trophies, besides storming to promotion twice with record points tallies for clubs like Foggia, taking them up into Serie A with a group of good but not incredible players. Then there are those that hate him simply because he has attacked more times a system that, effectively, would be condemned by the justice few years later.

Having said that, if you know your football, it will only take you 10 minutes to spot a team coached by Zeman. The same goes for sides coached by Sacchi or Guardiola. Maybe there's a handful of other coaches you could say that about too. But no more than that.

But I find it a lot harder to recognise other coaches' teams by their style of play, even if those coaches are very successful. I think that creating a recognisable style of play and at times inventing a new brand of football is a massive compliment for any coach, regardless of what trophies they win.

The reason I'm saying all this is because that year we had a new fitness coach. He was a short, stocky guy from Puglia. He was down to earth and always had a smile on his face, but he also had the courage of his convictions. He claimed he had studied the fitness coaching techniques that Zeman had used at Foggia and said he wanted to implement them with us.

Raffaele.

We all called him Raffa.

I don't know who he knew at the club and why he was suddenly tasked with the first team fitness coaching. I think he must have a been a certified fitness coach. And I'm sure that he offered to do it for free to prove himself.

Anyway, he implemented his methodology.

And it was very simple: in every training session we would have to do 100 jumps, lifting our knees up to our chest. It was 10 sets of 10 and you had to do all 10 in a row without stopping and only touching the ground once. So, as you landed, each landing was also the push off for the next jump.

That was it.

Easy. But we'd do it every time, no exceptions.

And you'd do well to really picking your knees up to your chest, otherwise he'd be chewing your ear off.

We wouldn't do all of the sets in one go. But he would halt the training session at random and we would do a set of 10 reps.

Then training would resume, be it a game, tactics, whatever and then, all of a sudden, boom, another 10.

And we'd keep doing that until we reached 100.

Every training session, week in, week out.

The first few times we did it we could barely walk for the amount of lactic acid that built up. You could milk us for gallons of it.

But then it gradually became routine, it no longer hurt, and it was no longer a strain.

In fact, we'd even bust out 20 of them in the pre-match warm-up on a Sunday, just before kick-off.

Raffa's jumps. They were iconic.

But here's the good part.

With no explanation, without warning, just out of nowhere, a miracle occurred: we could suddenly play at 100 miles an hour. For the whole game, whatever position, whoever the player and whatever their age.

We would walk all over the opposition because we were always first to the ball, always quicker, with an intensity on a whole other level to all of our opponents. Every time.

Fitness-wise we had them on toast.

Of course, that didn't sort out the finishing ability of the guys who had no eye for goal, but when you are always half or a full second ahead of your opponents, it's a big advantage and half of your problems go away.

It was quite simply a miracle. Unexplained and inexplicable.

After the first few matches, once we'd seen evidence of what a big edge it gave us, whenever Raffa told us to do our jumps, I'm sure that more than half of us always did a few extra reps.

They had become like a drug.

Raffa would tell us to do 10, whereas I'd do 12 and so would Ricki. Knowing Maxi, he'd definitely go as far as 14.

Sometimes such unexpected and surprising phenomena teach you that small victories, little signs and evidence of success help to build motivation above and beyond any effort.

They are marginal gains but very tangible ones that make the difference. You can talk theory all you want and be inspired by lots of different concepts, but nothing motivates you quite like clear, tangible results. Nothing inspires success, like success. Even if the successes are very small.

I learned it a few years later. And Raffa came to mind.

No one, I'm telling you no one – and I'd bet my mortgage on it – would have given even a penny to him at the start. Nice guy, but no credibility.

He had come up from the South with the idea of replicating some of Zeman's training methods.

Yet he was the fitness coach who achieved the best, most tangible results I'd ever seen in all my years playing football and in the quickest, most striking way.

A few years later when I was coaching the national football team within my company, I used those same methods myself to great effect (finishing 2nd and 3rd in two World Cups) with teams which were good, but at least 7-8 teams were really looking stronger in the tournament and way more organized. All things considered that was an acceptable amount of work for the gang.

For as long as I played football, even in the over-35 second tier in Switzerland, I always did my jumps either at the start or end of training. Maybe I wouldn't get to 100 but I'd do as many as I could. In fairness I am not sure about what my cartilages would say if they could talk, but that's another story for later.

I don't know what happened to Raffa. Every time we meet up as a team, every 1-2 years, we always recall that nice little man and wonder where he is and what he's up to. But no one has ever been able to track him down.

I even tried googling "Raffaele", "jumps", "fitness coach" and "Foggia" but to no avail.

It's a shame.

I would like to tell him that he gave us an edge in case I didn't tell him enough back then.

I believe we should always recognize the small things that make a big difference instead of always looking for the next great big deal. They exist and they have value. I hope that he really made a splash because he showed so much to everyone despite starting with so little.

A SAD SHOOTOUT

When April comes around in Bologna you start to feel the pull of the riviera. And when the girlfriends come to the ground on a Sunday in flip flops and a vest top, it means they're stacking chips that soon or later they'll want to cash. It's like a uniform, a sign of a revolt. One that screams, "Look at me, I'm a martyr to your footballing gods, but I won't forget it."

There was only one thing that could come between that week's work or study and a day at the beach: a seventh or eighth tier match at 3pm on a Sunday in some small town in the middle of nowhere, where at best they'd serve a coffee at the bar and the average age was pushing 70.

It was a slightly ungrateful situation and thinking about it today, it sounds like a punishment that our girlfriends really didn't deserve.

A league season feels endless. Ultimately you play 34 games in an 18-team league and it seems impossible that you'll make it to the final day with everything on the line.

It was the last day of the season. We were fourth from bottom and we faced the team who were just a point below us. So, a draw would suffice. But if we lost, we were down. It wasn't only a season of Sundays given up for football matches, the details and results of which no one would remember, but we were also in danger of getting a kick in the teeth in our last match.

Another tragedy was occurring on that day, 1 May 1994. We were in the car, the blue Clio as ever, Maxi, Ricki and I heading to our final league game. Meanwhile the San Marino grand prix - that run on the Imola's circuit, just a few kilometres from where we were playing our match -was going on and it witnessed the tragic death of one of the best drivers of all time, Ayrton Senna.

The game kicked off a bit later than usual, at 4pm, so we were still in the car on the way to the ground listening to the radio at 2:20 when the news came through. As soon as we got there, I remember we stayed in the car for several minutes while we followed reports, but they didn't give much hope to the listeners. A few minutes later the helicopter was already on its way to Bologna's Maggiore hospital. They got there quickly, but there was nothing they could do. We went into the dressing room and that's all anyone could talk about. Everything was happening just a few km away from us and that made this event very closely connected to us: it was happening in real time, live, in our town. The coach was shaken up, but despite that we had a game to play and it was all or nothing.

It's always shocked me to think that the line between life and death is so thin and that the passing could be so quick: one second you exist, the next you don't. I've always been a logical person and I try to give a sense to things by using logic. This was something I couldn't explain, and it made me feel uneasy. Years later, first when my grandmother died, then my father and later my mother right before my eyes, I stopped trying to grasp what we can't and we shouldn't understand.

There is no reason and no logic to understand that exact moment of the passing.

And I stopped asking myself questions I had no answers for.

I think Maxi did likewise when he lost his brother, but I never asked him.

I never had the courage to.

Maybe it was the same for Ricki when his dad had hoisted the sails for his longest trip.

So, while I was troubled by thoughts about how thin the line is that separates life from death, the presence from the absence, the everything from the nothing, I told myself that there was a long way between survival and relegation – it spread out over 34 matches. But when you're in the dogfight, whatever had happened over the course of 33 matches, you always come back to the fact that there was one moment, a single match that would decide everything and determine whether you'd have all or nothing.

I had never been relegated. Nor had Maxi or Ricki. This could have been our first time.

It was brutally hot, the sort of heat that I often shut down in. Let me play at minus 15 degrees Celsius. But no more than 25.

Ricki was struggling too, but luckily Maxi was there and he could boot it into touch better than anyone. I remember clearly feeling at half time that even another minute of play would have been impossible for my body. At the break I took an ice-cold shower while still in my kit and went back out on to the pitch completely soaking wet. It would help.

I barely remember anything of the match, I don't even remember how I played, if I played my part and whether or not we deserved the result. But in the end, it didn't matter whether we deserved it. All that mattered was not losing and how we did so was irrelevant.

I remember feeling in agony because of a heat I'd never experienced before. The air was so thick it wouldn't even fit up your nostrils and I remember thinking that's where the expression "gasping for breath" comes from. It was like breathing something solid.

I do however remember very clearly the moment that separated us from relegation, as we were saying.

All in one moment. That thin line.

The final whistle.

I could tell you exactly where I was on the pitch and from where I watched Maxi once again clear it towards midfield. Before the ball touched the ground again it was over.

0-0.

We were safe.

I remember that I didn't have the strength to celebrate, maybe not even to stand. I might even still be lying down on the bench in the dressing room with that soaking shirt on my forehead, had it not been for the desire to get out, to finish that season and that day which would forever go down as a sad day in the world of sport.

LIGAMENTS

Maxi, Ricki and I did our knees seven times between us: 5 ligaments, 1 patellar tendon and 1 meniscus. We only had 6 knees to choose from.

Ricki brings the average down. I take it up.

If you allow six months of rehab for each of those injuries, we spent a combined total of six and a half years recovering from surgery.

But we always came back.

On our "3-man weekends," when we strut our stuff on the ski slopes over a couple of days, it always brings a smile every time we let out a grimace of pain when we have to stand up again. It's worse in the mornings, when we've just woken up and we have to drag ourselves out there, shuffling along like penguins without moving our ankles. It takes a few minutes before we gain full rotation of the malleolus.

Then you're nearly there and, to be honest, after half a jar of Nutella, we're ready to race the Streif all in one go. More or less anyway.

We're good skiers. Technically I'm a cut above the others thanks to the 13 winters I spent in the mountains when I lived in Geneva. But I was the best skier even before that. Ricki and Maxi are decent too though.

Come on, guys, I'm kidding. We're all very good.

It's fairly incredible to think that guys with seven surgeries across six knees spend months planning one weekend in the year, only to meet up and see who can best handle the Streif or the Lauberhorn in

Wengen's downhill. The latter has a section through the woods which feels endless and you take it all at top speed and, just when you start to feel the quadriceps bursting into flames, you promise yourself: "Never again."

Then you come back to base and say, "That was cool, shall we go again?"

We've skied Sestriere, Porte de Soleil, Kitzbuhel, Garmisch and so on. We deliberately choose the World Cup slopes, the hardest ones to ski.

Try yourself rocking "The Swiss Wall" between Avoriaz and Les Crosets with more than 90% gradient - where to take a breather, you stay on your feet and rest your shoulder against the slope.

But we're there, rain or shine. And we really go for it.

We always set off with grand designs, planning to tear it up. Then we're all in bed by 10pm in front of a sci-fi film. We get a pizza delivered because "I reckon we're best off resting that knee tonight and putting some ice on, so it feels better tomorrow."

But despite all that, we can hold our own.

We might wear an extra knee brace here or there, but we hold our own.

When you rupture your anterior cruciate ligament, it's a case of deja-vu.

The first thing you experience is excruciating pain for ten minutes. It only lasts for ten minutes but it feels like a lifetime.

Twenty minutes later you no longer feel a thing, because it's already swollen up like a melon and it feels like it's been wrapped in several layers of brown packing tape that you need a pair of pliers to cut through. You try to move your knee and your whole leg moves with it, as a single unit. You go to move your quad and your calf moves with it. Only Ricki's knee didn't swell up a lot, because apparently his break occurred in a staggered sequence and not all in one go. So it was almost as if he didn't notice it, but any time he went to change direction he could feel that his tibia and femur weren't very stable.

Then you go home and you continue to apply ice to the knee for 12 hours, just to get through the night. It's a relief and you can put weight on the knee the morning after, but it stays locked between a 120- and 150-degree angle, with a bare minimum of extension and flexing capacity. You can even increase the rotation if you try, but you need to do it slowly and allow the liquid inside the knee to flow and compensate for the movement.

The next morning you go to see the orthopaedic surgeon, who usually performs two movements. First there's the "drawer test" to see if there is any translational movement of the tibia on the femur, by pulling it forward and pushing it back. Then there's the "jerk test" where the knee is placed at 90 degrees and slowly extended, creating a subluxation of the tibial plateau. I've done it so many times that in the end I had them explain it to me.

But the crazy thing is he had already diagnosed—it was ruptured knee ligaments—in less time than it took for you to read this paragraph.

That's is, if you're lucky.

If you're less fortunate, the doctor sticks a syringe in your knee – a needle thicker than a juice-box straw – to remove the liquid that has flooded the joint capsule. And that isn't a nice feeling, because it doesn't last the length of a vaccination ... it lasts several seconds.

Then the diagnostic part finishes and the worst bit begins.

When I did my cruciate in '92, the doctor who operated on me was the most famous in Bologna and without a doubt one of the three most famous in Italy.

He was a pioneer. He had reset Roberto Baggio's knee. And boy Baggio's knee had been in a state.

Back then they were just bringing in and trialling a new technique called the "Kenneth Jones procedure" which seemed very well suited to sportsmen and allowed for a record recovery time of 6 months.

That's if everything went well of course.

They would take a strip from the tendon in the kneecap and then insert it in place of the anterior cruciate ligament, creating a hole to feed it into the tibia before fixing it with two pins – basically two large flat spikes with more teeth. One pin on the tibia and one on the femur.

They needed to do a good job on the hole because that was crucial both for the ligament's stability and tension. So it needed to be done well, as I said.

Back then you would spend 3 days in hospital because they had to drain a small amount of liquid after 2 days. Then off you went, back home on crutches.

That leg would not touch the ground for 4 weeks. Not once.

And you have to respect that rule. You have to ensure that leg never touches the ground - no ifs, no buts. Because if it touches the ground, that could undo the whole procedure.

I've had plenty of surgeries and every time, looking at the knee, listening to it and feeling it in the days after the operation, there comes a time when you worry that it will never go back to what it once was. You can't really feel it. And even though you might have already been through it, this time it seems impossible that this weak thing that doesn't move could once again withstand running, sprinting, changes of direction and striking the ball with power – that power and whip that allows a cross to curl away towards the penalty spot so it's almost perpendicular to the goal.

"It would no longer be possible." I remember thinking that every time, after every operation. And you really believe it too.

You remember you've done it before, but this time the feeling is really awful. This time it's no longer possible.

The fear grips you. You can't control it.

Then day after day you secure small victories.

One step further.

One more stride in the pool.

One less centimetre of swelling.

The first full rotation on the bike.

All small victories, one at a time. Every day.

It's the small victories that keep you motivated. It's today's victory that drives you to achieve one tomorrow as well. It's like an Everest that can only be climbed one step at a time and that's the only way of getting it done.

I think rehab teaches you a lot about life.

You start in a difficult state and you think you can't do it, but that's just when you discover the determination that takes you to that first small victory. You have to earn every little bit of progress. Above all you can never stop, because every bit of progress is so small that the only way to consolidate it is by continuing to increase it. You are forced to keep pushing forward, to think only about progress and your next daily victory.

There never comes a time when you have truly finished and it's always like the first day, when you have to earn that centimetre of extension or a few degrees of flexion. You need the same bite and determination. You must never forget your first day because if you stop and think you've made it, it's game over.

It's brutal at the beginning.

Basically, you have to turn a rope into an elastic band. You struggle for every degree of flexion and then one degree after another, with every new centimetre you make progress.

There's pain. And lots of it.

After a month, with rehab sessions at least 4-5 times a week, you aim to achieve 80% mobility. At the end of the month, you take your first steps and do away with the crutches.

You walk.

Once you start to walk you eventually achieve full extension, because it's natural you recover that when walking and forcing yourself not to limp. After three months, from one day to the next, with the growth in muscle tone, the physio can then put you on the treadmill. But this time would be different from all the others when he asked you to walk at 4-5km per hour. All of sudden he tells you to change the settings to 7 or 8km per hour.

That means only one thing: running.

It was the moment you were all waiting for. Running.

It was the sign that you might have made it. I say might have because until you kick the ball and it goes exactly where you want it to and until you control it without the ball getting away from you, you're not there yet.

But that was still a few months away.

When he said to me, "Set it to 7 km/h," which meant a light jog, it gave me goosebumps. My time had come.

You knew it would eventually come, but you're never truly ready. It's like when they award your team a penalty. For a split second you think "Great!" Then you think "Shit, now I've got to take it." Have you noticed that the penalty-taker never goes over to celebrate with the teammate who's won it? It's not bad form, he's just nervous. And superstitious.

The guy who won the penalty has done his bit. For the penalty-taker, the journey has only just begun.

But there is no other option, there are no more excuses - they tell you to run, and you can only do one thing: run.

And you run like it was the first time ever.

You feel a bit blue as you begin to run when you realise that you'd never really forgotten what running means. You run thinking about the last time you ran before the injury and you remember that stopping running was a punishment, not a choice. And so you fully deserve to reacquire the technique.

You are running.

You smile and look at the physio who knows exactly what you're thinking: "You see? I am running!" He smiles at you while thinking "Go for it, my friend."

You feel a bit heavier on the treadmill and you feel the sound of every step, but you like realising that for a moment your whole body, your entire weight, can be on one leg, the same leg that only a few short weeks earlier could only stay straight with the aid of crutches. You quickly realise that your hips have got their shape back and you transfer your weight.

You find rhythm and feel the pace.

Get me back on the pitch. I'm running.

I can run. I have to tell my parents.

The first time I did my cruciate was at the end of April in my fifth year of high school. I didn't go back to school after surgery because with two hours of physio a day at Casteldebole, plus a half-hour commute each way, I decided to study from home. My mother drove me every single day. Every day. She would come back from work at 1pm and then come and pick me up at 4.

I don't know how I would have got through that period without her and to think she wasn't a big supporter of my obsession with football. They were "11 men in their underpants chasing after a ball." To be fair, it's hard to disagree with her. But she was brave, and she gave me courage. She was stubborn and she gave me determination. She never gave up, my mum.

When I got home at 4:30, I would try to study. I would grab a book, lie on the bed and try to read. And I would be out like a light. I didn't really properly study after that. I did my high school leaving exams based on what I could remember. In the philosophy oral exam, the teacher asked me to choose a topic and I said, "I would like to talk about Nietzsche" not for a precise preference but that was only because it was the last subject we had studied before my injury, so I still remembered some of it.

But he had a copy of the Communist „Manifesto" on the table (the most popular left wing party newspaper) and said, "OK, well, let's talk about Marx's materialist doctrine instead". It didn't go well. It wasn't even for political reasons – something I've never been particularly well versed or interested in, neither before nor since – but simply because I quite literally „slept through it" upon returning from a physio session.

I was used to collapse on the bed, exhausted.

The treatment was brutal.

When you're doing it, it doesn't seem that hard. But when you finish the session, you've got nothing left to give. Especially if you need to study.

Anyway, I went out that day and said to my mum, "I ran". There weren't many mobile phones back then (besides the ones that looked like a portable phone booth) and so I had to wait until 8 that evening for my father to get home so I could say to him, "Dad, I ran".

Then my running became more fluid and my calves, hamstrings and quads got their tone back. The teardrop muscle was always the last one for me and in the final weeks we focused on that small piece of muscle which, even today, is smaller than its equivalent on my other leg.

Then came the day of the machine test: the isokinetic test. That machine tells you whether or not you're fully recovered.

The machine is what separates you from getting back out on to the pitch.

I was intrigued by that machine. It looked like a leg extension machine, but it was fitted with a screen and hooked up to a computer. Plus, it offered unbelievable resistance, not only when you extended the knee but also when you flexed it. In fact, in order to use it, they had to tie your ankle to it so it pulled and made resistance both during extension and flexion.

They told me that machine, just like a number of others that were used in the physiotherapy clinic, had been invented and built by Mr Technogym.

He must have been an American.

Indeed, the entire physiotherapy facility, which had once been a countryside estate and went on to become one of the largest of its type in Europe, began to be filled with lots of equipment that bore that name in a soft yellow font against a black backdrop. That's something I noticed because I couldn't think of any football teams that wore yellow and black. I gave it a lot of thought, but nothing came to mind. (Wolverhampton, to tell the truth, plays in yellow and black and in Italy Juve-Stabia is as well showing those colours, but at the time I didn't find any).

That guy had talent.

Seeing lots of injured players use those machines I thought it was a wonderful thing to help players recover from injuries, helping them come back stronger than ever. Who knows how many players worked their way back to fitness thanks to those machines?

So, what was the priority for an injured player? Returning quicker and stronger than ever. I felt like those machines changed the lives of footballers, and therefore mine too.

A brand, a series of products with an important mission.

From that day on, I thought about Technogym as those machines that help doctors and physios to get footballers back in action. I didn't know what fitness was. Let alone wellness, I had always played sport outside, so I didn't go to the gym. All that mattered to me was going back to playing. And just as those machines had helped Baggio to get fit again, so they would do likewise for me. I think that's something that Mr Technogym and his staff must be very proud of.

I was lucky enough to meet Mr Technogym many years later. He wasn't American. He was actually born 30 minutes from Milano Marittima where I used to go to the beach.

He is a very smart man, unique in his intuition, vision, curiosity and principles. I thanked him for changing the lives of so many sportsmen who had returned stronger than ever. Myself included.

The day of the test, after a good warm-up, they tied you to this machine fitted with a computer, to measure whether or not the power you had generated in terms of extension and flexion in the injured leg was the equivalent to the amount generated by the other leg - the healthy limb, in doing the same exercise. At that stage it was all a case of recovering muscle power because the knee had already regained movement and stability, so the decision on whether you could resume playing football essentially came down to whether or not the injured leg could match the healthy one in terms of generating power.

The first test didn't go well. I still had a 30% difference. I started to work even harder. Every day.

Three weeks later, with only a 10% difference, I could begin running on the pitch and get a feel for the ball again. It had been about 5 months. "Mum, as of next week, let's take my boots with us."

From there the return to action is fairly quick and if all goes well, within 2 months you're ready to play matches again.

There's a magic moment when you realise you can do keepy-ups, control and strike the ball as naturally and as accurately as ever. It's just a moment. It's like a spark that runs from your brain throughout your body.

It's like when you score a goal.

It's a moment in which you feel everything, all in one go, yet you understand consciously nothing.

That moment is worth each and every one of those 6 damned months. It's worth all the sweat and it rebalances all the tears. It all becomes worthwhile.

At that moment, you're back.

COMEBACKS

The first game back from my first injury, the ACL on the right knee when I was 18 years old, I came on a ground I knew very well - the Savena pitch at Pontevecchio sports club. I had played several tournaments there ever since I was a kid and in one of those, when I was with the Giovanissimi, I was chosen for a select XI to take on AC Milan's Giovanissimi side. I still have a plaque to mark the occasion.

So, I always thought that the pitch brought me luck.

In the middle of the first half a corner was cleared as far as 5 meters from the edge of the box, where I was. It was a very similar dynamic of the situation when I broke my ligaments, many months before. I didn't hesitate a millisecond. I struck the ball with my laces with all the strength that the machine with the computer could measure and with all the strength that all of Mr Technogym's machines put together could produce. And with a lot of good coordination.

And there wasn't only strength and power in that strike. There was also anger, frustration and pain. There was the disappointment and suffering of the first day of physio, the sadness of the first run and the disappointment of the first strength test. There was the pain of the injury, just two days after mixing it with a team of professionals that featured in the Panini sticker albums.

And there was hope.

That hope that makes you believe that things could go back to how they were.

And there was the courage that my parents had given me on every step of that journey.

When you strike the ball cleanly, you can hear it. It's a sound that you recognize instinctively. You don't process it rationally; you feel it inside. I remember the sound of that ball I struck purely with the outside of my laces, with a slight outside lift. As soon as you hear that sound you know that you've either scored or you've given the keeper a real problem. Luckily the keeper didn't even have time to see the ball. He didn't even try to stop it.

I was back.

Despite the procedure of a surgeon who was seen as a pioneer, that new ligament did not last as long as we'd hoped. Barely six months later I suffered my first twisted knee and I tore the ligament so much in two years that it became useless. Then with one final twist I also ruptured my meniscus. Later on, they would tell me that the hole they'd drilled to feed the new ligament through may not have been perfectly aligned. And just think that doctors from Japan had even come over during my rehab to see the outcome of this new surgical procedure.

I had my second operation with a different technique, in which they took two tendons called the hamstring tendon gracilis and semitendinosus and wrapped them together before inserting them in place of the cruciate ligament, albeit through a different hole. The operation was performed by the same surgeon that had worked on Maxi not long before and he had a very good reputation because he had also treated lots of basketball players.

It worked. Very well in fact.

And it is still solidly in place to this day, holding my knee together.

When I ruptured the tendon in my kneecap 10 years later, I went back to him. He was a man of very few words, but he always nailed the diagnosis, and he always had an answer.

One year in Geneva, I felt excruciating pain that almost prevented me from walking, and I suffered with it for four months. I was still playing football, but I couldn't understand what was causing the pain and ironically the more I rested, the worse it got. I would sit down for an hour in a meeting and I could barely get back up again. Even when I did, I was constantly limping around.

I went to three of the leading surgeons in Geneva with my scans. They were considered world-renowned surgeons.

One used to operate on professional footballers. Another one treated the Swiss ski team. They were all guys you needed to book an appointment two months in advance, so between booking it and when you actually meet them, you hope to still have the symptoms to show.

The first thing I noticed was that they all took a good look at the scans before they began the check-up. They all came to the same conclusion. There was an edema in the tibial plateau, but they said that couldn't explain the pain I was experiencing. But the more serious issue was the damage to the cartilage, especially on the side from which I'd had half of my meniscus removed - the medial ligament in my right knee. And they could do nothing about that and in any case, arthritis in the knee would have gradually given me more and more problems. But above all there was no treatment they could offer me.

There was no remedy to my pain.

They had no advice to give.

I got stuffed with anti-inflammatories and pain killers.

And so, I just had to resign myself to the fact there was no way of treating it. The pain would come and go.

That's it.

One of them, the last that I met, left me with a recommendation that felt like a slap in the face that I didn't deserve: "I think that at this point it's time to start thinking about a future knee replacement."

I've not cried a great deal in my life – you could probably count the total number on the fingers of two hands, which is strange if you ask me – but that's the truth. However, this was one of those times when that void overpowered all of my defence mechanisms. I remember calling Cinzia and blubbing something, but I couldn't get the words out. Stefano, a great friend of mine, called me that day. He is one of the friends that really listen to you. He just gets me and he, more than anyone, can get me focused on the three most important things in life. Which is why he's the guy I always turn to when I have to stop thinking about myself and get some fresh perspective. When I need to get back on an even keel and find a centre of gravity. However, I couldn't even get a single word out with him either. But listening to him helped me, because I was feeling blue and because good listeners also understand the untold and can spark you back into life.

He helped me unplug and restart and I decided that that idea, that recommendation was not OK with me. World-leading surgeon or not, I was not OK with that.

A few days later I spoke on the phone to a friend and former teammate of mine who is a sports doctor at ISOKINETIC in Bologna and the Bologna Club doctor. Luca, or "Doc" to the players. He gave me some hope merely based on the symptoms I described over the phone, but he said he needed to back that up with a check-up and a scan, so he wanted to see me as soon as possible. But in the space of 10 minutes of questions and answers I felt like he'd understood more than everything I'd been told up until then.

I went back to Bologna for an appointment, both with him and with the surgeon who had done my second cruciate surgery (the successful one) and also fixed the tendon in my knee cap a few years later.

They worked together from time to time back then.

Their appointments were the complete opposite of their Swiss colleagues'. First, they listened to my story and the description of what I was experiencing. Then they asked me hundreds of questions before going to work on my knee: touching it, listening to it, pressing it, pulling it and constantly asking me what I felt every time they manipulated it. They also asked me to do stretching exercises and observed the way the rest of the body responded.

I never understood what they were looking at.

That's when they started to give their opinion and thoughts on the matter and only then they would take a look to the scan. I got the impression that they needed the scans to compare them with the hypotheses they'd made from the physical check-up. That was the opposite of the Swiss guys, who looked at the knee to corroborate what they had seen on the scan.

I remember after Dr. Lelli had given my knee a good working over and before the scan he said to me, "Yes, your knees have worked very hard, they are suffering and the cartilage has certainly become lodged in a number of different places, but what you're now experiencing is linked to a trauma and a seriously overworked tibia, which could have a significant edema." And finally, he added, "I'll have you as good as new in 3-4 months provided you are consistent in doing what I tell you." Then he looked at the scan and said, "There you go, you see."

I was surprised by two things. The first was that they had all spotted the edema, albeit from the scan, whereas Lelli had diagnosed it by touching and working the knee. But even more than that, no one had set much store by the edema, certainly not enough to justify my pain, nor had anyone told me that something could be done to sort it out.

It was exactly the same thing with my mate, Luca "Doc" Bini. The same process, same diagnosis, same prognosis, same hope, same plan: "Magnet therapy, every day, at night, for at least three months." Confirming the hypotheses he did over the phone already few weeks earlier.

Anyway, I ended up buying this little magnet therapy machine. It cost €500 and it's still one of my most prized possessions. I used to fire it up overnight, every night. Within a month the pain was a lot less and 4-5 weeks after that it had gone altogether.

Two years later I ran the Berlin half marathon in around two hours after five knee operations and with one thought in my mind, "Dear Swiss pioneer knee surgeons, you know where you can stick your knee replacement...?"

For now, at least...

THE PITCH AND THE PITCHES

A football pitch is a special place.

I've always thought that what makes a football pitch beautiful is the fact that it is clearly established in terms of time and space and yet within its boundaries anything is possible: any system, angle and ball flight. Anything is possible.

You just have to come up with it. And it's you who has to produce it.

The thin white lines demarcate the pitch. Some people see this as a limitation, whereas it makes others feel safe.

In any case the lines surround you, they enclose you, they give you bearings and act as a guide.

They define everything there is and everything that matters on the pitch, while everything that is not required and doesn't matter has to stay off it.

It is those lines, those thin honest lines, that separate everything that matters in football from everything else that is not a part of the game.

The pitch is honest. It's the great leveller. There's no scope for ambiguity.

Everything must occur inside that space, and within a specific timeframe.

There is a right place and a right time. For everything.

A bit like in life perhaps.

The lines on a football pitch are clear, visible to all, consistent and persistent. In the workplace, they serve like the strategies, the long-term choices. They have to be clear and serve as a benchmark and a guide for every plan and decision. Within those white lines you have to harness all of your creativity and innovation to create and own your game.

The game is always played by a team in a competitive environment; you never play on your own and you don't just pass the ball to one another for the sake of it. And there is no game without the opponents. In organizational terms, everything should be compared to a competitive environment; you should have an external benchmark. Basically, it's pointless to "talk to ourselves."

It's useless is to pass the ball to each other without an outcome or a result that is visible and tangible externally, that offers a tangible benefit to a client, or that improves the life of a consumer, eventually creating a competitive advantage. Practically, only passing the ball could even be a stimulating exercise, eventually for training purposes, but it doesn't help anyone.

A team has ultra-clear roles, and everyone needs to be the best at what they do and not just average at doing someone else's role. And you even train differently because goalkeepers and forwards mustn't operate in the same way. Everyone has a role and roles by their very nature are different.

Everyone knows who takes the corners and who goes up for them. Everyone knows who takes the goal kicks and the free-kicks, as well as where they come from and where they should be directed.

Everyone knows to rely on their teammates and the team as a whole, but they also all have individual qualities which must not be stifled based on other people's qualities. Every individual should be able to thrive.

And just like a penalty taker has a very clear individual responsibility, even though he's part of a team, and he takes the spot-kick on behalf of the team, such responsibilities are also very clear to everyone; there's no ambiguity. The team exists but it is made up of clear individual roles.

It sounds very simple. But it's not. In fact, it's very difficult.

The other thing that has always fascinated me is that on the pitch, during a game, the perspective constantly changes. Spaces are closed down while simultaneously, provided you're switched on, new angles emerge in which to imagine and to create. Sure, at times when you get to the by-line, it becomes very tough to spot space - options become limited and things become difficult. But we shouldn't feel desperate, because one thing is always true: there is always an angle and a line that connects you to the goal.

Always.

It's mathematics. Actually, it's geometry.

One option vanishes, another one appears. Skill and talent lie in spotting, in that moment, that perspective, or line, that others can't see.

In finding a solution just when others have lost all hope.

In always living with intensity the exact moment when if a door closes, another one opens at the same time.

The Football pitch. You can feel it.

You never look at it, but you always feel it.

And that feeling stays with you forever.

It's irresistible and indispensable and to this day I still can't help going out on to an empty pitch, walking inside and changing my angle and perspective. I sometimes recall moves from the past, too many to remember but they are also too striking to forget.

Like the first time you are handed a trophy as top scorer and you can still see yourself as a kid, smiling in a photo and you will never forget how that felt.

And every football pitch has its own story to tell, its own role to play. It's part of a line up.

It all started at La Barca when Maxi, Ricki and me, were around 6 or 7 years old, starting at the Bologna academy that had been created at that time. They even wrote a lovely article about it in the paper. On that pitch we learned the value of "smelling the grass".

Ca' Bassa was a 7-a-side pitch: my first pitch, where I played my first match, my first tournament. It didn't survive the urbanisation of the 1990s, but it will live long in the memory of us Pulcini.

From Pulcini to Esordienti, where in the winter we trained at the Stadio Renato Dall'Ara. Not inside the ground but in the square behind the Andrea Costa stand. I remember some wonderful matches on the concrete, sometimes covered in snow, but nothing could stop us. I well remember the most beautiful match ever. It was in a training session. There were Maxi, Ricki and me plus another 8-10 kids. The concrete was completely covered in snow and the cones to make the two goals, but we wouldn't stop. Our parents arrived to pick us up at the end of the training, one first, then three, then another five. They stopped around the square watching the match. Five, ten, then fifteen minutes passed but they didn't stop us. The coach as well didn't stop us. It was magic. No-one could have ever interrupted that happiness that was alienating us from anything around us. Then, suddenly, the lights went off. It was dark.

Everything was over.

It was great playing in the Dall'Ara because we used to change in the first team dressing room. They were anything but nice facilities back then, but they belonged to proper footballers, and it was exciting to think we could be a part of that team.

I skinned my knees so many times on that concrete, ripping holes in my tracksuit bottoms faster than my grandmother could sew them back up again.

Those two concrete areas didn't survive refurbishment work for Italia '90.

The Virtus in Via Valeriani, near the stadium, saw us move from kids kicking a ball around into a proper football team. We went unbeaten and became unbeatable. It taught us technique, formations and tactics. So much technique because the surface was a mixture of grass, rocks and clay and you never knew what was coming next. So, you had to hone your technique well to control the ball even just once.

But more than any other one, that pitch was where our first proper team was formed.

In that centre circle they gave me a big speech about my future as a professional footballer, which despite my best efforts and intentions, never came to pass.

The velodrome was surreal because it didn't have any stands but instead an inclined concrete track designed for cycling that I never once saw used. Despite that it felt like a real ground surrounded by stands on all sides.

The Arcoveggio was a really nice grass pitch for two months of the year and it was very treacherous for the rest of the time. It was the pitch on which Maxi, Ricki and I played more than any other. I played there between '92 and '98, while Maxi and Ricki played there for many more years – Ricki for at least another 10.

The Villanova, the Savena, the pitch at Castelmaggiore and the one in Corticella, they were the ones that hosted the most prestigious and competitive pre- and post-season tournaments. They were tournaments held at night under floodlights. The atmosphere was unforgettable because when you play under floodlights, it seems like the light is all for you. You are basically the main event in the neighbourhood at that time. Floodlights at night are captivating. They create those four shadows on the pitch that are all different from one another.

But above all, night games completely dominate your entire day. There's not a single moment during the day at school when you're not thinking about the match that night. It dominates your mind and everything else becomes an afterthought: it helps you get through hours of Latin lessons. And sometimes you can't understand why Pirandello is so arrogant as to distract you from that evening's semi-final at the Villanova tournament. Please give me a break let's talk about it tomorrow! ... Provided we don't lose.

And the next morning you come to class limping, courtesy of that defender who wanted to stop you at all costs. That would be all you and your classmate who sat next to you would talk about for the first hour.

We've all definitely played on every pitch in the local area and at least half of those had a decent enough surface, whereas probably less than half survived the move to Astroturf.

Either way, they all had the same shape, the same lines and the same rules. Like a blackboard. Like a painter's canvas. A sheet of paper upon which to write a new story – Sunday's story.

They are all the same and they have defined borders but they have no limits. They are written and rewritten every time, at every match and every tournament.

And the page is filled with a story that might just excite the reader.

But in truth it is only unforgettable for those who write it.

CHOICES

In September 1993, Maxi, Ricki and I were all back together again. We would have gladly played together forever. All three of us had opportunities to play at a higher level and we had the ability to do so, but we were growing up and we knew the time had come when two or three big decisions would determine how our lives would pan out. We were almost 19 after all and we were well on the university path, in three different directions.

We decided that it wasn't worth breaking the band up just for the sake of playing 2-3 levels higher. And that football and friendship could no longer be separated and were now non-negotiable. We kept playing on that team for as long as we could.

Those decisions led to hundreds more training sessions and games together, so many unforgettable moments, and they helped to forge a lawyer, a vet and an engineer.

They created our time machine. The blue Clio.

I graduated in 1997 aged 23 and two months later, from one day to the next, I began working in Rome. That was February 1998. I left the team at the end of January. And I went back every now and then for training or to see a couple of games.

Maxi and Ricki got their degrees and kept playing.

I started playing again both in Rome, for the company's national football team that I have also coached, as well as in Geneva in the over-30s for six years.

We played together again in a few tournaments, including three separate editions of the World Cup that was run by the company I worked for. In Switzerland, Germany and France. I also coached the team for a time between my first and second ligament injuries.

Maxi and Ricki kept playing until they were 40.

Ricki still plays in a variety of different tournaments but he's always moaning about his back and his knees. Only last year I went to watch him play in a 7-a-side tournament between lawyers. It's amazing to see how aggressive lawyers become when they play football. You'd think "the law" would keep them honest, but you soon realise that football is "above the law."

With the Bologna lawyers' team, he's even made it to the national final at least three or four times. I think he's even won a couple.

Maxi is in incredible shape. Even today he nips in before you see him coming.

It's been so long since we last played together and we must do so sooner or later. I always dreamed of formally retiring from football, of organising a testimonial with friends and former teammates.

Ideally, I would take our Bologna Esordienti side from 1987 and match them up against the 1994 Croce Coperta Turris team. But I would add in some friends that have been along for the ride with us, like Silvio, Stefano, Luca, some of my colleagues, some of Maxi and Ricki's friends, plus other friends from football tournaments and battles down the years.

It can't only be one match: it needs to be a whole tournament. Maybe all three of us could play at least one half with all of the different teams.

That way we're sure of winning. But we wouldn't go to Burghy afterwards, as it's no longer there. But that doesn't matter. We could no longer have burping contests and throw chips at teenage girls.

But that's not important.

Football defined us, developed us and shaped us. And football has left us with so much more than that.

WHAT REMAINS OF FOOTBALL

As you get older, you gradually come to realise that your brain works at the same speed that it did when you were 12 and you expect your body to do likewise.

But your body falls a tenth of a second behind, which then becomes half a second, then it becomes a full second, then it becomes a malleolus fracture.

In my final years as a player (or what remained of the player I once was) I was living in Geneva and played in the Swiss over-30 league, a safe haven for lots of former professionals. In my team alone there were three guys who had played in the Swiss Super League, the country topflight.

At 36 I also brought home a Swiss Cup. In one of my games, I was told that Stephane Chapuisat played for the opposition. He was 39 but he was someone who had scored more than 260 goals across the Swiss top division and the Bundesliga, along with 21 goals in 103 caps for Switzerland... Just saying...

I would never have recognised him – with the greatest respect to the Swiss team of the 90s – but my teammates from Plan-les-Ouates pointed him out to me.

But we won the match, and we took the cup home with us.

I also played centre forward. I don't know why but in that team, they decided I was a striker. It must be because once I got moving, I could take out the opposition defence in one fell swoop, just like when I was a "Pulcino" (under 10). Isn't it ironic that at 35 I would make a difference using the same skills that I had when I was under 10? While In between I had to reinvent myself, learn new positions, work on my strengths and make up for what didn't come naturally to me.

Maybe that's how life is too. At first you have natural qualities that move you along and give you a push in the right direction. But then in order to be accepted at school, socially and in the workplace, you need to reinvent yourself to fit the system and make up for your shortcomings, because those shortcomings will end up holding you back.

Then there comes a time when you get so fed up that you no longer wish to do what you don't want to, or to improve your weaknesses. So, you go back to what you want to do, to what you've always known how to do, to what comes easily and naturally to you.

At Plan-les-Ouates we had a ground with about 6 pitches and the training pitch had a surface like the grass at the Dall'Ara. It's fairly standard practice to play on facilities like that in Switzerland. I must've seen all of five or six pitches that weren't the same standard as a Serie A surface.

A few seasons after that I played for Lancy, which was the team closest to my office – fairly practical with two young kids at home. Twice in the space of one season I had to call my wife and say, "Get a taxi to the pitch, I can't drive and I need you to take me to A&E." It was 10pm both times and it wasn't ideal with kids aged one and three at home. Luckily though we had a live-in au pair back then and that gave us a lot of flexibility. So I even had the luxury of a few injuries and overnight stays at the A&E.

That was further proof that my mind and body were now working at different speeds, as I broke my ankle and the tendon in my kneecap in the same season. I didn't require surgery on the ankle, while the knee was much more of an issue. I remember when she took me to hospital the second time she said to me, "It would be nice if this were your last ever injury!" Who could argue with such sound advice?

Beneath her eloquent, sound advice lay a tacit, more colourful version: "For god's sake, babe, give up the football! Do you not see that you're no longer up to it and you're doing everyone's head in? Over the last six months you've seen the female doctor at A&E more than you've seen me. Do you now realise it's time to move on?"

She used to pretend to be serious, but I think she really struggled with how I couldn't grasp the situation. Yet she was hoping that this time around I'd get the picture. My wife has always been a very hopeful and positive person.

And I did indeed retire that day. I was almost 39.

I secretly played a couple of matches with my colleagues, because I was lucky enough to basically have a stadium in the Herzogenaurach campus where I work. I never told my wife and she never had a go at me for what she found in the laundry basket – no doubt a full dirty football kit. Some things just aren't worth arguing about and it's wise to give them a pass, but I am sure she noticed.

I never did get to have my testimonial, but I've always promised myself I'll organise it one day. When I mentioned it to my wife, she suggested I play it on Xbox, as it would probably be safer. Who can blame her?

I always wondered what remained of football, come the end of 34 years of training sessions, matches, teams, coaches, pre-seasons, injuries, operations, rehab, teammates, referees, success, joy, pain, frustration, and physical and mental suffering.

I've got no doubt about that. Along with so many memories, some of which I've pieced together in this book, there are three things that will forever change what I see as my football and my life.

The first is friends and friendship.

Maxi and Ricki are friends for life: they played with me and were best men at my wedding – teammates in football and in life. They've always been there and they always will be. Football brought us together and life has taken us down different paths, but nothing has ever divided us.

We always understood and accepted one another despite our big differences. We're so different in terms of the way we live our lives and yet so similar in appreciating who we are and how we approach things. Differently.

We have cried laughing, gasping for air, and we have wiped each other's tears when there were no words with which to console one another.

That's who we are. We're still the same. Whether on the football pitch, in the blue Clio, on the Streif or in front of a jar of Nutella which is always gone too soon – blame Ricki for that!

We had our hiccups, and we had episodes that may be debatable, but I want to believe that our friendship goes well beyond the episodes.

The three of us share a bond that goes way beyond just us three. It includes the teams we played with. Guys we shared dressing rooms, hard graft, shouts, insults, and cheers with. The vast majority of our friendships were forged in a team and go beyond that team, beyond the football and beyond any single match. Naturally work and school introduce you to nice new regular acquaintances. But I've never had stronger friendships than the ones I enjoy with guys I passed and received a football from thousands of times. It's as if football the metaphor – in which you give and receive the ball – is there to remind us of what friendship is all about.

I think sometimes people see friendship as a possession. They define friendship as spending time together and people talk about "inseparable" friends. I realise this when I talk to my children about friends, when trying to figure out the value and dynamics of friendships. We decided that the number of playdates or sleepovers with someone has no bearing on the strength of the friendship. Nor do the notions of possessions and proximity either. Friendship should give you time and take up time. They're like an elastic band.

And when I hear people talk about "inseparable friends" I always smile because I believe the opposite is true. I believe true friends can actually be "separable" but without anything ever changing.

"Separable" but nothing comes between them.

That was how it was for us. Separated but nothing would change between us, nothing would change us and nothing would come between us.

So much has been written about friendship and we certainly won't be the ones to change its meaning and importance. But when puddles of mud, mistaken referees, undeserved defeats, epic victories, slides on the grass, silent dressing rooms and races through the snow in weather so cold it will freeze your bum cheeks all combine, then friendship certainly takes on whole new colours and dimensions.

It's not that the essence of friendship changes, but when you go through all that together, perhaps you are laid back enough to move past any misunderstandings. They do still happen of course, but they can't really leave their mark on a painting already so full of vivid colours.

The second thing are the feelings and emotions that have become lodged in an irrational part of our minds, which will never leave us, yet come bursting forth to the surface every time the senses feel them.

The seal fat (Dubbin) that we used to apply to our kangaroo skin boots in the 1980s and '90s had a texture and smell that will never leave us. But it's not just the senses the smell stimulates, it's the memories it evokes too. It reminds you of the night before a game, when it was time to check your boots and shine them. That's when you started to get in the zone and visualise the game.

Those feelings remind you of the build-up, the rituals and mental preparation for the game.

Once I got to the dressing room, the first thing I would do would be to take out my boot bag, remove my adidas World Cups (with 6 studs) or my Copa Mundial (with 13 studs) and place them under the bench where I used to sit.

I would leave them there to air out and let off their scent of seal fat while I put on my kit. They would be the first things I would prepare, but also the last thing I would put on. It was just my simple way of reminding myself that everything was ready. It would be a battle and I was up for it.

And I would only ever lace them up once I was on the pitch. While kneeling down. At one with the pitch, and with the grass.

The deep heat (called in Italy literally "Tiger's Balm") that we used to put on our quads and hamstrings on particularly cold days had a scent that immediately wafted throughout the entire dressing room. It permeated everything and everyone. It was like when my mum served up "tagliatelle alla Bolognese" and the smell of the ragout reached every last inch of the house. She didn't need to call me for lunch. The smell alone took brought me to the table.

The tiger balm was horrendous. You had to get through the first few minutes when every area you applied it to would become incredibly itchy.

But the smell stayed with you. Forever.

Walking through the tunnel from the dressing room was like a symphony. Sounds and vibrations that are part and parcel of football itself. That's why I always preferred the 6 metal studs because of the noise they made, even though technically I really liked the black ones with the white tips. A few years later adidas made black studs with metal tips – the pinnacle! They made the same noise as metal studs but they looked as nice as the black ones with the white tips.

Perfection.

The half time cup of tea was awful if I'm perfectly honest. It was too sweet and I'm not even sure it was actually tea.

But I used to love holding it in both my hands.

On those cold, rainy days when Bologna treats you to a steady drizzle that covers the sky and a fog that cuts through and weighs heavy on you, that hot cup of tea was the equivalent to a hug from mum when you came home from school after a bad test result.

It consoled you, it wrapped itself around you and gave you hope because there was still 1 half to play. And anything could still happen.

Because there is always a second half. For everyone.

A new start. A new moment only made of possibilities.

We've already spoken about the smell of the grass. The grass is everything in football. On some pitches it means you can definitely show off your skills. The grass will determine whether or not your control will end up one centimetre to the left or the right, which might mean the difference between scoring and hitting it wide. Between winning and losing, between living and dying inside. The grass and the dew will both determine the speed of that shot, hit from a standstill, but that with two skips across the turf it becomes almost unstoppable.

Before I used to go into the dressing room, I would first take a walk on the pitch. First, because that's what professionals do, so it was cool. Second, because there were some days when you needed to in order to pick the right pair of boots. Third, because you could see the empty pitch, big enough to see yourself running into the right space and small enough to curl that through ball away from the opposition defence and perfectly into the stride of your striker to finish.

I've never understood the move to Astroturf.

I mean, I get that it's practical – it doesn't require any maintenance and it provides consistent quality all year round. But guys, it's not football without the grass - its smell, it's honesty and it's truth.

The full-time whistle was always either a sense of relief or a falling axe. There was no alternative. It was a watershed moment because hope very quickly became either realisation and delight, or anger. But it was a definitive verdict and there was no room for ambiguity.

I always liked the full-time whistle because it's so sharp, decisive and brutal, yet honest. It closes the circle. I don't like to leave things unfinished and I can't live that well with ambiguity. It disturbs me. I love the clarity, the transparency, the honesty including the one that hurts, but that doesn't leave too much space for interpretation.

We could do with more full-time whistles in life, to move on and leave everything behind. To end everything and begin something new.

The third thing that stays with me is the importance of "giving everything" and doing so all together.

Every time.

That sounds obvious but it's not.

Football matches are cruel. They are limited in terms of time (90 minutes) and space (roughly 100m x 50m) and anything can happen in that time and space. But above all, everything must happen because whatever goes on before and after has absolutely no value. There is no after, there is no second try, nothing exists outside of it.

It's here and now.

Now or never.

In that limited time - just like a lifetime - and in that space, marked by the lines, everything has to happen. You have to do everything and give everything in that time. Because there are no second chances.

It's brutal and it sounds like a judge's sentence but that's the way it is. That's how football is unfortunately – or fortunately as the case may be – and so too is life.

And what's great is there's only one way of giving everything: do it every time.

You can't decide whether or not you're going to give everything today. It's not a contingent decision but a prerogative. It's an attitude.

It's impossible to give 100% in a match but only train at 50%. You can't discriminate between a training game and Sunday's match. You can't complete that shuttle run unless you give it everything and the same goes for those jumps. Always pick those knees up to your chest. Each of them. Every single time.

You can't pick and choose. You can't count selectively.

It's not like you give it 70% in training because ultimately, you'll give 130% on matchday. There's no scope for coasting when you have to give it 100%. The sum of 70% and 130% doesn't make 2x 100% in football.

Maxi was good at that. He never played a training game at anything other than 100%. Ricki and I learned it over time.

I remember my daughter's first gymnastics competition. She was six years old. Four runs in four different disciplines: balance beam, floor, parallel bars and pommel horse. They awarded podium places for each discipline, with gold, silver and bronze medals and then there was an overall points table with the total number from each discipline.

There were around 80 girls competing.

She didn't win anything. Nothing at all.

She was upset and we chatted about it. She wanted to win something, and I was delighted to see that it bugged her that she hadn't. I secretly revelled in her disappointment because as far as I'm concerned, frustration and suffering lead to desire and desire lays the groundwork for success, in whatever area it may be.

I used to take her to a gym on the other side of Geneva on Sunday mornings, where she would train with her gymnastics team between 9am and midday. It was a bit of a pain for me, but I turned it into something productive by using the time to work.

But I would watch her.

And it was obvious in those three hours of training that she would do the exercises as a break between a chat with one friend, or a game with another. She just did them for the sake of it. And not because every single exercise was the best she'd ever done.

When we got home after that competition, I said to her: "Kikki, I'm going to let you in on a secret... competitions aren't won during competitions themselves." She gave me a strange look.

I added, "Competitions are won during training."

She kept looking at me in a strange way. To be fair, it wasn't the most logical concept at first.

I then said, "You win when in a training session - every single exercise must be the best, the most intense and better than any other exercise you've ever done before. Every exercise must be better than your previous one and the best ever."

I finished by saying, "So give it 100% in training, at all times, in every exercise, every single second. But when you're in a competition, have no fear and just have fun and enjoy it. Never the other way around."

I thought she got it.

Around 4 months later, in the next competition, she won the lot. Gold medal on the beam, gold on the floor, silver on the parallel bars and silver on the pommel horse. They kept calling her up on to the podium for medals. She had more medals than she could hang around her neck.

And she won the overall standings. It was a lovely trophy.

I think she understood what you need to win, that attitude and that mentality that seizes you. That desire and that belief that wins you over.

Maybe one day you come up against competitors who are better than you or further along in their development. And that's okay too, provided you have given 100% and not only on competition day, but in every exercise in every training session.

I remember some football matches where I felt exhausted, but I would still walk back to the dressing room. I stood up in the shower and I even had the strength to go out on the Sunday night. Why? Why hadn't I given everything so I could no longer move a muscle? What good was it not running that extra yard and not tracking back? Then you end up wasting that extra yard on something useless after the game. I asked myself so many times how this could happen, and I always promised myself that it would never happen again. Never again. That in the following match I would have run that extra yard whatever it took. That extra recovery run, that extra yard, one more jump, one more sprint. I would no longer ever have the energy to get back to the dressing room. I would take my showers sat on the ground and I would barely be able to move come Sunday night, let alone go out.

Football makes you think life could be very similar. What does "giving 100%" actually mean? Do we realise when we're doing it (or not as the case may be)? Do we understand how important it is to have no regrets? But above all do we realise it in time?

If you still have something left to give, maybe that means you haven't given enough.

Watch out. Once the referee blows for full time, it's all over.

That's another thing football has left me with. That incessant, all-powerful voice that says, "Give it all."

Because once the game is over, there's nothing more to give.

EXTRA TIME AND PENALTIES

In all fairness this book, written in 20 days during April 2021, ended up here.

I never thought specifically about what to write, it just came out without thinking. Like when you are on the football pitch and you see a corridor no wider than a laptop screen, and you pull out an assist that no one expects. Not even you.

This book came out like this. Without thinking.

And for someone who thinks a lot it was a very new experience; I would say uncontrollable.

In fact, looking back at many years on the pitch, I realized that there are times when you can't think too much. It is a rule of the field, you need a free mind and it is essential to abandon yourself to your instinct and be guided by your heart. When you are on the pitch, you know that you have to play the diagonal towards midfield and you need to think about the next step in the rehearsed play. But taking a forward step in a split-second decision over the opposing midfielder, foreseeing a pass before it happens that leads you at full speed to put all the opponent's midfield on their backfoot, comes from instinct.

These were my best plays.

"Follow the force. Follow your instinct. Trust me." Star Wars is always right.

Then when the play ends you have to get back into your position and start thinking again.

And after the trance of the previous chapters, I thought that there are episodes that take place beyond the final whistle, and they must be celebrated especially if they close a circle that starts from afar.

In July 2021, while some friends and some champions were already reading the draft of this book, sending me thoughts and comments that I would never have imagined, we witnessed a European football championship that continued to tell the story of the magic of football, of team, of friendship, of the strength of the group, of humility, and of dreams that rise from the ashes of defeat.

The pride that grows stronger from the deepest humiliations.

I was 8 years old when I saw together with my father Italy win the World Cup in Spain in '82. From that moment on football entered my veins forever.

In 2018, Italy did not even qualify for the final round of the World Cup in Russia. My 8-year-old son will have no memories of that World Cup. It was by far the lowest point in the history of Italian football.

The Euro 2020, played in 2021, evoked once again the beautiful contradictions of football, and of life. It proved once again that there is hope, as Rai' wrote to me in his thoughts on the book. That there is a second chance for all those who want to believe in it and who are willing to question themselves, to continually improve, and to change. For those who intend to expect more from themselves than others think is possible. For those who have the courage to dream and to believe beyond all reasons, and to dare and take risks beyond calculations and predictions.

Obviously my judgement, as an Italian and Swiss citizen, is very biased. But I believe that Switzerland first and Italy later have demonstrated what it means to believe beyond all logic. What humility means. What the strength of the group means, putting oneself at the service of the team, showing what results it can lead to. What courage is. How you can win without showing off (indeed history teaches that it is better to fly very low first and better not to get a tattoo of the cup before having won it). How you can win quietly without humiliating your opponents. And last but not least, how a coach can create an environment, a mentality, and a level of confidence to believe the impossible. And when you believe it, then dreams really can happen. Anyone who loves football must be proud of this.

Switzerland against France gave us one of the most memorable displays of humbleness in recent years of football. France the reigning World Champion and on paper the strongest team in the tournament. And the strongest by a large margin. When in your midfield line up you have Kantè, Pogba, Rabiot and in front Benzema, Griezmann and Mbappè you can only win. And you must win, which is a bit of the disadvantage of being the strongest, on paper.

Switzerland, from leading early on by its own merit, went from a possible 2-0 by missing a penalty, to 1-3 in a matter of minutes. A partial score that would have killed anyone. It was a "coup de grace", you can't believe in a comeback when you play against the reigning world champions in a round of 16 of the European championship and you are down by 2 goals.

But that's the moment when you have to believe in it.

It is the moment that liberates the magic of the pitch, in which everything becomes possible. It is the moment in which, you cannot afford to start showing off on the pitch because you should show that you are the strongest only once you have won.

Yes, you can also be funny and very cool dancing and showing off while you are winning.

But you have to win.

The dance, do it later, once you have won.

If you win.

No opponent in our division has ever dared to dance on the pitch in front of Maxi. Because in the next corner you don't want to find your nose next to your ear.

Be that as it may, Switzerland little by little began to believe in it again. It didn't become disjointed because of those 15 minutes after the missed penalty. It came out at the other end. The "rossocrociati" narrowed the spaces, shortened the distances, improved the circulation of the ball. Everyone took their responsibility even with some risky plays. They had courage. They shortened to 2-3. Then scored for the 3-3. And after the extra time Switzerland won in a sequence of penalties that played fairly well in their favour.

What a joy Swiss!

I told Mattia on 1-3, "It's not going to happen, but if it does, I am stripping naked and I will go for a run on the street." I had made the same promise when Roma had to make the "remuntada" with Barcelona in the quarter-finals of the Champions League in 2018.

Fortunately, when Yann Sommer held Mbappé's last penalty, a very strong downpour came which gave me a sufficiently valid excuse, especially in times of COVID, to avoid running naked on the street.

Mattia was understanding. That's better.

But the house still trembles from the cheers of that night.

This is the best football, at least for me. The one in which the heart beats arrogance and hubris. The one in which talent can never be separated from character. The one in which humility always forces you to give your best and more, whoever the opponent is. That of the second chances, which do not happen by themselves but you have to create beyond of every turn of fate. "Audentes fortuna juvat"— Fortune rewards the brave. Fate is the friend of those who dare. I didn't say it, but Virgil.

Hop hop Suisse.

And then it happens that you can lose the quarter finals on penalties against Spain. The same penalties that brought you there have defeated you, but with honour, and with the team, Spain, that played the most consistent football of the entire tournament. With the same courage that brought you there. And with the same respect towards football and the opponents. The same respect which Spain demonstrated in turn against Italy in the semi-finals. And together with Spain, Luis Enrique. A great coach. And a great gentleman.

"Il Mancio" was 18 when Maxi, Ricki and I were in the youth team of Bologna, during our beautiful 8 years of age. He was our myth. Him and Marco Macina of the same age were the emerging talents of Bologna and Italian football. One came from Marche, the other from San Marino. So similar and with such different futures. Differences so small at the time, but over the years they became an unbridgeable abyss. No one at the time would have said for sure which would have had a more successful football career.

Marco stopped at 26 with only 13 appearances in Serie A and no goals.

Mancio made his debut at the age of 16 in Serie A, becoming one of the strongest attacking midfielders in the history of Italian football, 541 appearances in Serie A, 56 goals, 36 appearances for the national team, 4 goals. He has won 2 Italian Championships, 6 Italian Cups, 2 Italian Super Cups, 1 Cup Winners' Cup, 1 UEFA Super Cup.

Following that he became one of the most successful Italian coaches both in Italy and abroad, winning 3 Italian championships, 4 Italian cups, 2 Italian Super Cups, 1 English Cup, 1 Premier League, 1 Community Shield, and 1 Turkish Cup. Then, with the Italian national team, he created a group that won the European championship becoming a knight of merit of the Italian republic and a great official.

Il Mancio.

He was "one of us."

He, who has always had a mixed relationship with the national team. Good performances, but not exceptional - or in any case never at the level of those with his Sampdoria, paired with Gianluca Vialli. The goal twins.

With Bearzot, perhaps one night too many in New York could have been avoided. With Vicini he played more in the 1988 European Championship but without ever making a difference, and without ever exploding. In Italy '90 he was the only one among the 6 forwards who didn't play, with the rise of a new generation of number 10s, including Baggio.

So not only was the 2018 Italian national team "in the ashes" but also Mancio came from a very complicated relationship with the blue shirt. I would say of love and pain.

A challenge.

On some occasions I have had the impression that some challenges are not chosen, but they choose you, they look for you and they follow you. They are those challenges that come from afar, that emerge from the past. These are the challenges that become indispensable for those who, at any cost, do not want to leave open a tab with the past.

Il Mancio had a circle to close.

In these cases it is no longer a matter of convenience. Roberto Mancini had many clubs in Europe that would have more than tripled the contractual value that tied him to the FIGC.

But the real challenge has nothing to do with the economic incentive. There is only one incentive.

To win.

Certain choices choose you. Victory, too, sometimes chooses you.

Mancio has taken a team reduced to ashes and re-founded it through many quality young players, forming it day by day, game after game.

Giving it a vision, instilling confidence, showing results. One after the other. Up to 34 consecutive useful results and 17 consecutive victories, always looking at the next game instead of the success in the previous one.

Mancio has come full circle, transforming the frustrations of the past into the victories of the present, and into hope for the future. Calmly, patiently, without ever losing control of the interactions with the outside world, or of the locker room. He chose the challenge, and the challenge chose him. In his match with the national team, in this relationship, he earned a second chance, he earned his extra-time.

He created a group obtaining the maximum focus in the performance, and the maximum fun as a group. There is nothing better than such a cultural and behavioural context in team sports.

He reminded me of our team, Maxi, Ricki, and me, and our friends at the time of the youth teams of the Bologna academy. We had found friendship on and off the pitch, and we had discovered the life inside the game. It was our whole world. And it was our whole life. So much that even today we get a little excited every time we happen to be together again, on the pitch. During the European Championship, in July 2021, it happened twice in two consecutive weeks, which for those who live 800km away from each other is a great fortune.

On the evening of the European Championship final, a match that started badly and ended in triumph, we were in Italy with lots of friends and lots of children, on the beach. A dinner that was an excuse to share the final with many friends and with our children, finally our chance, after the disappointment of 2018.

Immediately after the last Donnarumma save it was a sprawling celebration. Mattia, me, our little and big friends.

The definition of "messy cheering" comes from my friend Silvio based on his personal experience of traveling to see Roma in the UEFA cup. You recognize messy cheering when "overwhelmed by the crowd, devoid of any sense of space and time, you find yourself several rows below the one in which you were sitting at the time of the goal, hugging a guy with a moustache you've never seen before, without knowing where your glasses went and how far you will have to travel to get back to your seat. But above all, you will never know who the gentleman with the moustache was."

In our case, a few minutes after "the messy cheering", we could no longer find the children but we soon discovered that they had undressed, and after a run on the long beach of Milano Marittima they had thrown themselves into the sea, in the dark of the night. Mattia was the promoter, obviously... He too had an unfinished business regarding the "messy cheering" promised by his father during the Switzerland-France.

The circle had also come full circle for us. And not only in relation to the cheering, but we had the second chance to understand the victory and understand its strength, energy and colours. Together.

In the extra time of life there is always the hope of overturning the result, of changing the fate, of strongly believing beyond any logic and beyond any reason. The possibility of dreaming and expecting much more from ourselves than what others believe of us. The will to always go a little beyond what seemed the best possible only yesterday. The opportunity to write and rewrite a story that never ends.

Until it really ends.

Printed in Poland
by Amazon Fulfillment
Poland Sp. z o.o., Wrocław